The Last 48

The Last 48

Survive and Thrive
by
Banking Faith and Love

Lee Carrick

*All book profits to Christian family ministries
and veteran support organizations

ISBN: 979-8-218-86272-5

Independently published by Such a Time LLC
LeeCarrick.com

First Edition (2026-5)
Printed by Amazon, Inc., in the United States of America

Cover designed by Katherine Benson
Cover art "Kingdom Perspective" painted by Lee Carrick

Editors: Blair Parker, Paula Peckham

Author Photo: Mr. Johnson, Sgt, Orange County Police Department
Back Cover Photo: Alisha Cory Photography
https://alishacoryphoto.com/

Dedication

All praise and gratitude to

Jesus Christ,

my Lord and Savior

Consider it pure joy, my brothers and sisters, whenever you face trials of many kinds, because you know that the testing of your faith produces perseverance —*James 1:2-3*

Contents

Preface

I grew up in the small town of Winter Park, Florida, in the sixties. I was a regular little kid who liked to draw and paint, ride my bike, catch fish, swim in pools, play on the beach, and enjoy the sunshine. In many ways, I haven't changed much in the past sixty years.

My story revolves around key life choices I made and the resulting promises I kept. It begins with meeting a pretty girl, Suzanne, on an unplanned blind date when we were seniors in high school in 1974. While in college, we both accepted Jesus Christ as our Savior in 1978, the best choice we would ever make in life. After college, we married in 1980 which was our second-best choice in life. We enjoyed a lifetime of love for over forty-two years. She was my best friend, and we did everything in life together.

During our life together, I served in the U.S. Air Force, the National Aeronautics and Space Administration and the Central Intelligence Agency. After military retirement, I completed a second career in private industry where job titles and accolades were important in industry but a distraction from what is really important in life. Of all the titles I had in my life, the undisputed best was being Suzanne's husband and follower of Jesus.

Despite being in excellent health her entire life, Suzanne made the jump to Heaven unexpectedly after only six days in the hospital in December of 2022. Since then, I reflected and analyzed our life with one another and stitched the seemingly unrelated actions and words together into a message I need to share with the world. The time allowed me to capture what I learned as a man, a Christian, a husband, a father, a military officer, a businessman, and a widower.

What I now realize is the love I banked for Suzanne and the faith I banked in Jesus, compounded for 48 years. I was able to draw on these "banks" to survive a traumatic life event and thrive in moving forward with a new purpose in life.

I also believe banking faith and love can help a person survive any traumatic, life-changing event, and build a new life to make a positive impact on the world.

PART 1

BUILDING THE LOVE & FAITH BANKS

ONE

Beginnings

Suzanne and I grew up about fourteen miles apart in the quiet suburbs of Orlando, Florida (quiet then, not so much now). We had similar experiences as children in Central Florida as our hometown changed over the years.

As the population grew in the fifties and sixties, housing developers purchased large parcels of inexpensive land and used bulldozers to remove the tall pine tree forests and dark green palmetto bushes that covered the ground. Thousands of acres of working orange groves fell to make room for new housing developments.

Narrow streets in straight lines formed tight boxes around small house lots. Landscaping consisted only of heat-resistant centipede grass—a dense weed that grew quickly—but only the front yard was covered, rarely the back.

House layouts were simple one-story cinderblock houses with the floor about eighteen inches off the ground. Enough space to run plumbing under the house and provide Florida critters nice shelter out of the sun and rain.

Walls of concrete cinder blocks and window frames of iron withstood the high winds of annual hurricanes and flying debris from other storms.

Wood plank floors were hard and typically covered with wool rugs to soften the impact on feet. Tiny white moths nested in the rugs and flew around the room anytime of the day, while cedar-lined closets chased moths and insects away from clothing.

Bedrooms were small and grouped at one end of the house. One bathroom was typical in these houses; two for the rich folk.

Kitchens were all natural wood cabinets with wrought iron handles from a John Wayne western wagon train. Enough room in the kitchen for the mom and maybe one other adult, but no table. I avoided the kitchen in those days because if I misbehaved, I was within striking distance.

Before microwaves, the kitchen was also a place to get warm quickly from the oven that was used most of the day, feeding a constantly hungry family.

In the hallway was an oil furnace that provided heat for the rest of the home on the rare days of cold weather (below sixty degrees), a major improvement over coal-fired furnaces. Fifty-five-gallon drums filled with crude oil sat atop two concrete cradles about four feet above ground in the backyard. The oil ran through a copper tube to the inside furnace via gravity, and the furnace had to be lit with a match every morning; they were too dangerous to run at night while the family was asleep.

Many families enclosed a carport with windows to allow for air circulation on hot days to ensure comfortable Florida living; air conditioning was nonexistent, even in commercial buildings, in the sixties. When it was hot in Florida, which was a regular event, I'd laid flat on my back in cutoff shorts on my house's concrete floor to stay cool.

Neighbors were kind and looked out for each other, and people were always outside: tending their yard, washing cars, and sharing the latest gossip over the backyard fence. This was the world where Suzanne and I were born.

***

Suzanne's dad, Terry Purifoy, was born to a modest family in Texarkana, Arkansas. When World War II was raging, he enlisted in the US Navy after graduating from high school. During the Normandy invasion, he operated a landing ship that delivered tanks and heavy equipment on Utah Beach under heavy fire. He was one of the lucky ones to survive, but the horrors of war would eventually take its toll on him. After the war, he returned to work for the Cotton Belt Railroad as a clerk. In 1956, he was promoted to sales agent and transferred to Orlando.

Her mom, Dorothy English Purifoy, found a job in this new town as an office manager for the Minute Maid beverage company. Her parents purchased one of those cinderblock houses on Kipling Drive on the west side of Orlando in the College Park neighborhood in 1957—a typical mid-century modern house painted light blue with three bedrooms, two baths, and a one-car carport.

A few months after her parents arrived in Orlando, Terri Suzanne Purifoy was born on January 15, 1957, a Tuesday, at Orange Memorial Hospital, on Orange Avenue in downtown Orlando. The hospital was constructed in 1918, had only 258 beds, and did not have a maternity ward when Suzanne was born.

Her brother, Stephen, was five and a half years old at the time and finally figured out why his mother grew bigger so quickly. He thought the family was fine before Suzanne arrived, and sharing a living space with a noisy baby sister was not his idea of fun. Her bedroom was the smallest, with the larger one going to her older brother. Marile, who lived next door, instantly became her best friend for over ten years.

Suzanne was a daddy's girl and followed him everywhere. Fritzi, their tan dachshund, followed them, both with his fat belly dragging through the green centipede grass.

Based on photos, Fritzi was like a big watermelon with tiny legs. Her parents loved dogs and participated in dog shows when they first got married.

Terry loved poinsettias, which Suzanne helped him tend to over the years at home. Old black-and-white photos show her dwarfed by magnificent poinsettias that were two or three feet taller than her. Like most families who moved to Florida in the sixties, her dad quickly planted orange trees, called fruit trees then, in his yard, and Suzanne also helped him tend the fruit trees and pick the oranges when they were ripe.

Her daddy loved the Atlanta Braves Major League Baseball team, and since Florida did not have an MLB team, the Braves were the closest team to Orlando. Games were broadcast infrequently because sports were small, and shows of broader interest consumed the time slots on the three available channels—if the bunny ear antenna worked, and it wasn't raining too hard.

It was a big deal when the Braves game was broadcast. One game day, Suzanne sat on an orange vinyl day couch with her daddy in the Florida room watching the game. She didn't initially understand the game, but all that mattered was that Daddy liked this game, so she did too. Watching those games with Daddy was some of her happiest times as a young girl, even though the television's sixteen-inch black-and-white screen was low definition by today's standards.

Orlando grew rapidly in the sixties, and neighborhoods expanded around the Purifoy's house. When Suzanne was in elementary school, the Orange County School Board was redistricted, utilizing new schools that had been built. As a result, she attended five different elementary schools during her school career. Most of her classmates lived on her street, but some she would not see again as they were moved to different schools. At an early age, Suzanne learned how to handle change and make friends quickly; maybe this prepared her to be a military wife.

Suzanne was a Brownie Scout in Mrs. Ball's third-grade class and even kept her Brownie handbook, in which she wrote her name and phone number—CY3-7038—on the inside front cover. (I called that number so many times, I can still remember it.) Suzanne wasn't nostalgic; she lived for today and always marched forward. But she retained a few things that were important to her, such as her Brownie and Girl Scout Handbooks, still in their plastic protective covers. Her Girl Scout sash shows the words "Citrus Council" for the girls who lived in the Orlando area, and. next to it is a Cardinal patch, which signifies her troop's mascot.

Interesting that she and I would live in Virginia for twenty-eight years, where the cardinal was the state bird. She earned many merit badges, such as Backyard Fun, Camper, Collector, Cook, Dabbler, Foot Traveler, Gypsy (which made me chuckle), Health Aid, Housekeeper, and My Troop.

I hope those troop leaders realized the positive impact that they made on Suzanne and all those other young girls with the activities and times they spent together. Suzanne always reflected on these days fondly.

In 1966, her parents moved to a brand-new home in a new neighborhood about 10 miles west; it was a big upgrade with 1,400 square feet and a two-car garage. The large garage easily accommodated a washer, dryer, and hot water heater, which was the norm in Orlando homes in those days. The move put Suzanne in yet another middle school and was within walking distance of Evans High School. Leaving Marile and her friends was difficult, but her new friends would make an impact on her for the rest of her life.

The houses on her street, Indialantic Drive, were new, and all the transplanted kids wanted friends just like she did. Three of her new neighborhood girlfriends had strong Christian mothers who guided her faith in Jesus early in Suzanne's life. These amazing moms, Bev, Dot, and Helen, lovingly cared for her during middle school and high school. They knew about her parents' alcohol and anti-depressant addiction issues, so Suzanne was at their homes constantly, playing with her friends in peaceful environments. And those three moms, with Jesus's love in their hearts, cooked for her, watched her swim in their pools, played with her in their backyards, took her to movies with their families, and even took her on vacations with them. One of her friends recently told me Suzanne "basically lived with us during the day and slept at her parents' house at night." As a young girl, it was all Suzanne knew, not fully understanding why her parents were different than her friends' parents.

Bev taught Suzanne to sew, and she excelled with that skill, one day sewing her own wedding dress. This is just one example of many where I believe the love of Jesus in those women's hearts gave Suzanne her constant smile. And she loved those girls, giving them nicknames such as "Stanky Birdy" and "Ron Jon." For if Suzanne really loved you, she made a special name that only she would call you. Those aliases stuck for a lifetime, and those girls, now women in their sixties, would always laugh and smile when Suzanne called them by those nicknames.

Suzanne and her brother Steve fostered the typical sibling rivalry, and she managed the bedroom boundaries like an army sentry. When she started middle school, her dad's alcoholism grew worse, and her parents' marriage struggled. Home life was tough on her in high school as well, but she rose above it and was a good student, athlete, and friend. I wondered how she could get such good grades with constant chaos at home.

Suzanne's friend Debbie played softball, and seeing the obvious connection to her love of major league baseball, Suzanne started playing the sport at the Pine Hills Boys and Girls Club. Debbie's mother drove them to practices and games, where Suzanne played second base and was proud of her batting skills. Her coach, Mr. Lane, was a Florida State Trooper, and Suzanne said he was a good man and a great coach during this time in her baseball career.

An older girlfriend, Kathy, lived next door and was on the Evans Tennis Team. Suzanne respected her and learned how to play the sport as something else they could enjoy together. Her parents were not happy about Suzanne slamming the tennis ball against the garage door for hours at a time, but she persevered. She practiced consistently and tried out for the Evans High School girls' tennis team, which she was selected on her first attempt.

In typical fashion, Suzanne committed herself to this new endeavor and was undefeated in 1973. She also befriended Nancy, who was a year older and an excellent player on the team. Nancy was kind, a straight-A student, and an outspoken Christian who became a positive influence on Suzanne, and she would always mention Nancy when we reflected on our time in high school. Suzanne had many friends, including the big names of the boys' basketball team who won the Florida State Championship in 1975.

One player was Daryl Dawkins, the star of the team. He was a polite young man and always called her "Miss Suzanne." She loved that guy and was so proud of him when he joined the Philadelphia 76ers the year after he graduated from high school with her. You may know him as "Chocolate Thunder" because he broke basketball backboards with thundering dunks in the NBA. He was always a good man, likely because he too got his start in a simple small town with nice people.

Unfortunately, Suzanne's daddy's alcoholism worsened when she was in high school, and it broke her nineteen-year-old heart when he died. I was working in a grocery store unloading a truck when she found me and told me about her dad's passing with tears in her eyes. I'll never forget that moment and don't think she ever really got over losing her dad. She only spoke kindly of him and would tell stories of what they did together. I could tell by her voice and the look in her eyes how much she loved him and missed being with him. I never openly told her, but I always strived to fill that love gap for her throughout our marriage.

***

Eleven months after Suzanne arrived in Orange Memorial, I was born in Baltimore, known as "Ball-more" by the locals, and heavy snow fell that December night in 1957. My father was employed by Bell Atlantic and tired of working outside during the winters. When his company sought volunteers to transfer to Orlando, Florida, he jumped at the opportunity.

In the summer of 1960, my parents loaded me, my two younger sisters, and their belongings into the family sedan and started the two-day trek to Florida. They purchased a canary yellow and baby blue cinderblock house in a small neighborhood, which bordered Lake Bell.

My young life revolved around Lake Bell. A few neighbors who lived on the lake would let the kids play in their backyards and swim in the lake. It was a natural spring-fed lake that turned a tea color due to the tannic acid from the multitude of cypress trees that surrounded the lake. My friends and I spent every possible hour at the lake, fishing sometimes but mostly swimming. Usually harmless but often daring each other to jump off the roof of the houseboat or see how far we could make our bikes go into the water by pedaling off the dock.

As we swam, we saw gators slowly swimming in the reeds headed toward us. We would shout and throw rocks and oranges at the gators, and they immediately turned away, so we continued swimming. We never told our parents about all the shenanigans because we knew they would never let us swim in Lake Bell again.

Back then, my parents fed me breakfast, told me to get out of the house, play with my friends, and not come back until the streetlights turned on at dusk. My friends and I, and my sister Bonnie, made up our own fun. When we weren't swimming in Lake Bell, we fixed and rode our bikes, played tackle football in an empty lot, dared each other to climb to the top of the tall oak trees, and built forts in the surrounding woods of pine trees and huge oak trees.

I didn't know anyone who played organized team sports, and I wasn't even aware they existed. Because of this, I learned to be independent at an early age, which would benefit me for the rest of my life.

My parents attended St. Paul's Methodist Church, which Mom made my two younger sisters and I dress nicely for; I hated wearing that bow tie. I also disliked Vacation Bible School because I wanted to be swimming at the lake with my friends. But I learned to sing the song "Jesus Loves Me," which I still remember today. I was fascinated about the Bible stories of Daniel and the lion, David and Goliath, and Jonah and the whale.

When I was six, my mom enrolled me in Cub Scouts. About ten boys met in one kid's mother's Florida room for meetings, which used to be a garage. She was wonderful and taught us little boys how to do crafts, say the Pledge of Allegiance, and how to work together. I can still see the poster of President Kennedy on the wall with the words, "Ask not what your country can do for you, ask what you can do for your country." Funny how a big concept like that can stick in a little kid's mind; it was my first realization of the importance of honoring my country, which I still retain today. His words made me want to be part of something bigger and better than myself.

Cub Scouts led to Boy Scouts, and I was blessed to be in Troop 224. A doctor who owned a lot on Lake Killarney built a real log cabin for the troop. The older scouts were responsible for the meetings, and they ran a tight ship that an army drill instructor would be proud of. We raised the American flag at every meeting, said the Pledge of Allegiance, and stood for uniform inspection.

Since it was warm most of the year, we camped almost every month in the pine tree forests that surrounded Orlando. I learned how to prepare a campsite, pitch a tent, dig a latrine, and use a compass. We learned how to chop wood, build and tend a fire, cook on the fire, and clean up afterward. Merit badges were a big motivation and encouraged me to canoe, provide first aid, be a lifeguard, iron clothes, sew, hike fifty miles on the Appalachian Trail, and many more life skills. Leadership was taught at all levels, and I learned it was an honor and a responsibility to serve others by leading, never to be used for personal gain. Many sound leadership traits were formed in my young mind as a Boy Scout, which guided me throughout my professional and personal lives. Perhaps the most important lesson was the importance of self-sacrifice. Learning at a young age to care about others more than myself was a powerful lesson I retained all my life.

My dad taught me how to shoot a pistol by sending me under the house and into the attic to shoot pesky rats and squirrels that were unwelcome visitors. After pulling the trigger, my ears rang for hours, but it was worth the effort. It wasn't a fair fight, but their relatives kept trying.

One afternoon, my dad surprised me with a Honda 50cc motorcycle to ride in the woods with my friends. The first time I started it, I lunged forward, crashing into the side of his prized, but somewhat old, Cadillac. I can still see the huge scratch in the light green paint and the look on his face.

When hurricanes hit, we held towels over the windows to keep the rain from blowing inside the house as my mom mopped the concrete floor. When the eye of the hurricane passed over our house, the sun broke through, and my friends and I ran outside with my friends until the other side of the hurricane arrived, and we escaped back inside our houses. After the rain stopped, we rowed small boats around the block and swam in the lake that had overflowed. I loved growing up in my house by the dense woods and brown lake.

Eventually, my parents sold their house on Lake Bell in 1970 and moved to the west side of town into a new neighborhood. There were no lakes or trees, just flat sand, and I was heartbroken. But this brand-new house in Pine Hills had central air conditioning, and in the back of the housing division was a working orange grove that spanned hundreds of acres.

Since it was a new neighborhood, making friends was easy because all of us lost our early childhood friends while moving. The other kids had ten-speed bicycles, and I wanted to be cool like them. My father always told me if I wanted something I had to work for it, so I was determined to get that ten-speed and found a job selling newspaper subscriptions for the Orlando Sentinel when I was twelve years old.

My boss was a hippie with long brown curly hair, a dark beaded necklace, a beaded handmade bracelet, a tank top exposing pipe cleaner arms, bell-bottom jeans, and bad posture. He drove me and a couple of other kids, jammed in a small tan-colored foreign station wagon, every day after school and on Saturday mornings to sell newspapers. He took us to apartment complexes and told us he would be back in an hour to retrieve us for the next drop-off. I always wondered what he did while we were working but knew it was best never to ask him. No need for me to be an accessory to a crime at such a young age, and, worst of all, I would lose my job making twenty dollars a week.

When I was thirteen in 1970, I landed a dishwasher job at $1.40 an hour in the tiny restaurant in the corner of the Rexall Drug store in the Pine Hills Shopping Center. The only requirement was I needed to be fourteen years old, so I immediately told the store manager, "Yes, I'm fourteen." And he never asked my parents my age. I don't think he even cared if I had parents as long as I showed up every day. The manager grinned and told me to be at the store the next day at four o'clock. I wondered about his grin as I peddled my bike home. It was the same grin a guy would display when he caught a critter in a trap under the house.

He gave me the key to the front door of the drugstore and left before the store closed, probably to meet his girlfriend. I mopped, cleaned up, turned out the lights, locked the door, and then slid the key back under the door into the store. And no one ever bothered me on those nights. I turned my bike light on and pedaled home around 9:30 p.m. My parents didn't keep track of me; I just rolled where I wanted.

A year passed, and I heard the local Winn-Dixie grocery store was hiring baggers for $1.65 an hour. After school, I pedaled the trusty ten-speed to the store on West Colonial Drive, seeking to talk to the store manager. As I waited in the store office, a short man in his fifties with bushy black hair with thick, black-rimmed glasses, wearing a butcher's apron covered in blood, and an unlit cigarette in his mouth, asked what I was doing in a gruff smoker voice.

"Looking for a job as a bagger. They pay $1.65."

He lit his cigarette and, peering at me behind the smoldering cigarette, snarled, "I'll pay you $1.85 to work with me back in the meat market. It's air-conditioned, you know."

I immediately agreed, with no clue what the job entailed.

"Be here tomorrow," he said.

The next day, I met the store manager's assistant to obtain my timecard. She asked if I was sixteen years old. Of course, I said yes.

"Good, go to school and get a work permit, and bring it back so you can start."

My heart sank; surely my high school would look up my records or, worse, call my parents. The next day, I walked slowly into the administration office at my high school. I asked the grumpy, old lady with gray hair at the counter how to obtain a work permit. She asked, "Are you sixteen?"

You know what my answer was. She handed me the blank work permit, which I quickly completed before she could ask any more questions. She signed it and handed it back to me. My heart was beating wildly, convinced I would land in prison if they caught me. And it was a great job, one of my favorites of my life.

The butcher job taught me a new skill and a lot about life during the four years I worked there in the meat market at Winn-Dixie. I had a crash course in women, dating, marriage, raising kids, complaining wives, and the cost of living. Some of the lessons totally shocked me, and I hoped my mother never overheard the older men talking about life. I wore a long white coat, white hat, and white apron, which were mostly blood red by the end of the day. That gave me a cool vibe for a guy, similar to scars to prove a guy was tough.

Those older men were great to me and treated me like one of the guys. My new boss, Jim Bennett, was one of the best bosses I ever had. He knew his skill, worked me hard, and always watched out for me. I still remember some of his infamous life quotes, which can't be used in public. I learned a lot about people and leadership from that early relationship with Jim. I stopped calling him Mr. Bennett after my first year, and he liked it that way.

I worked all four years of high school and had to quit when I started college in the fall of 1975. And they never found out my actual age.

As a teenager in the seventies, Pine Hills, Florida, was a great place to grow up. Neighbors watched over the kids playing throughout the neighborhood. Most everyone I knew went to church. Televisions played the National Anthem every night before they stopped broadcasting at 11:30 p.m. Natural beauty was everywhere I looked, and the sky was always brilliant blue, dotted with large white clouds from horizon to horizon. Torrential rainstorms cooled the blazing sun almost every afternoon in the summertime.

It was a simple time that shaped Suzanne and I, and one day, we would build a life together around the same principles.

TWO

Our Adventure Begins

In the fall of 1972, my first high school crush, appropriately named Karen, abruptly dumped me for an older man of sixteen. I found out the hard way as I pedaled my 10-speed bike with the warped back rim past her house as she kissed a guy sitting on his 1966 Chevy Chevelle in Tripoli Turquoise paint with dual white racing stripes. After two weeks of utter despair, I vowed to take action; never get hurt again and get revenge by dating every girl possible in our grade. Retrieving the previous year's yearbook, I marked all the girls' pictures that appeared like they had a pulse.

My sixteenth birthday neared as I feverishly restored the 1968 Ford Galaxie 500 convertible my father dropped in the driveway for me to get running and restore. Between my dad and trial and error, I worked hard to rebuild, replace, and repaint everything possible with that car. Still the most fun car I ever owned, it was the second-best thing my dad ever did for me. The first was to teach me to never say, "I can't."

The restored old car became the "Red Convertible" to everyone and glistened like new, quickly becoming a chick magnet. Mostly because it was the only convertible in school, except for one unpopular girl's dirty Volkswagen Bug that wasn't a real car. The Red Convertible was the perfect car for the revenge tour I was on, and those high school girls agreed to go on a date with me only to ride in a convertible.

My favorite destination was New Smyrna Beach; the Red Convertible often packed with seven bikini-clad girls and a couple of guys. The new white canvas top was always down, and my 8-track HiFi blasted Bachman-Turner Overdrive and Deep Purple tracks.

Every chance I got, I passed that Karen girl's house who broke my heart, the one who started the revenge tour in the first place. I burned a lot of forty-cents-a-gallon gas working my way through the alphabet in my yearbook. But soon, I would meet a pretty brunette whom I would take for a ride, whose name ended in "P" and concluded the revenge tour forever.

Our high school, Maynard Evans, named for a local pharmacist, held the annual Sweetheart Pageant in the gymnasium in February of 1974. My buddy Greg, who owned a nasty fast AMC Javelin, slid smoothly into the gym with me. We welcomed the break from classes and the opportunity to check out the girls in the pageant. Trying to be cool at sixteen, we climbed to the top of the wooden bleachers where the cool guys hung out. Huge fans in the upper windows attempted to remove the heat but acted instead like a convection oven. A teacher announced each girl's nominating sponsor and the girl's name. Soon, I saw a dark-haired girl in a shin-length white dress with dark blue polka dots walk onto the stage.

As she stepped to the middle of the stage, smiling, she slowly spun her dress in a single circle. I asked Greg, who grew up in Pine Hills, who she was.

"Suzanne Purifoy," he replied

I didn't recognize her or her name. Why I remembered her, and no other girls in the pageant, was a mystery.

About five months later, I was on a double date with Greg and his long-term heartthrob. A friend of ours walked past our table with his date. I saw the side of his date's face and thought I recognized her, but I couldn't remember. She wore navy blue-and-white houndstooth slacks and a navy blue, short-sleeved cable-knit sweater.

"Greg, who is THAT?" I whispered.

"Suzanne Purifoy … she's on the tennis team," he replied.

I remembered him telling me her name back in February at the pageant.

The rest of that evening, I thought about how good those slacks and sweater fit Suzanne and, more importantly, her smile. Greg must have noticed my interest in her because he and his girlfriend hatched a scheme several weeks later.

That October, unbeknownst to us, Suzanne's best friend, Keri, and my best friends, Greg and Rick, conspired to get Suzanne and me together on Halloween in 1974. The plan required friends to meet in the parking lot next to the Burger Chef restaurant to attend a haunted house as a group. All the gang gathered and talked in the cool evening air. When it was time to drive to the haunted house, our friends quickly drove away, leaving Suzanne and me in the now-empty parking lot. I introduced myself and asked if she wanted to ride with me.

"Sure, let's go."

Halfway to the haunted house, the brake master cylinder leaked fluid, and white smoke slipped out from under the car hood. Realizing my brakes would fail soon, we caught a ride with Rick in his grandmother's orange Mustang, with no air conditioning and windows that did not roll down.

With it now too late for us to go to the haunted house, Rick drove all four of us to the outskirts of town and parked next to an orange grove. Suzanne and I crawled out of the miniature back seats, glad to have blood returning to our legs again.

We walked across a grassy field to a small hill while I talked for hours with this girl I had never met. The discussion was effortless, as if I had known her for years. I'll never forget her standing in the moonlight: red hooded sweatshirt, straight-leg Levi jeans, white Tretorn tennis shoes, long dark hair, and a beautiful smile with a hitch on the left side. Soon, we were dating regularly.

On most days, I met Suzanne in the school parking lot and walked her to her car. One sunny afternoon, she wept. She said she really liked me but had awful news. With a hitch in her voice, she said her dad was an alcoholic. She expected that news to make me break up with her because of this. She could have told me her dad was Stalin, and it would not have mattered. I immediately told her I didn't care, and I wasn't going anywhere. I still can see the broken look on Suzanne's face as she peered directly into my eyes and stopped weeping; that was another key moment in our relationship, bonding us more and building more trust that afternoon.

In the spring of 1975, we danced at our senior prom at the Contemporary Hotel in Walt Disney World. That may seem corny today, but it was big time in Orlando in the 1970s. The night was wonderful, and I deeply liked this girl. Suzanne was different: fun, kind, and happy.

As we danced, the band played one of our favorite Marvin Gaye songs. NO, not that song! It was "What's Going On?" I would remember that night and that song forever. We spent many nights on lighted dance floors with loud music, and people having a blast singing and dancing. We laughed and danced every chance we got. Suzanne was becoming the best friend I'd ever had.

Neither of us had much money, so we improvised. Shopping malls were popular then, and a new mall had opened on the east side of town. Fashion Square Mall soon became a regular hangout for us as we walked and window-shopped for hours almost every week. Despite being crowded with shoppers, it became our special world, and it seemed like we were the only two people there. I still remember walking, holding hands, and laughing with Suzanne. Always laughing.

Another favorite and inexpensive place to be together was the drive-in movies, which allowed customers to bring their own food, and admission was usually only $1.00 per person. For us, the drive-in was a special place where we could live in our bubble. She packed sandwiches and sodas in a cooler. And being the romantic that I am, I selected a different drive-in in Orlando each time; it was a good location to take a nice girl on a date. Our favorite was the Holleanna Drive-In in Winter Park, Florida, with its row of talk palmetto trees lining the entrance.

In the winter, when the mosquitoes subsided, I would bring a blanket for Suzanne and leave the convertible top down. Huge images filled the four-story-high movie screen we were watching while the scratchy dialog and muffled music crept out of the well-worn metal speaker hanging on my car window's glass. The big picture with little sound didn't matter, as we only periodically glanced at the screen while talking about every topic high school kids could imagine.

The numerous freshwater springs were also regular destinations for us, and, best of all, it required the girls to wear bathing suits. Eventually, we switched to Daytona Beach and New Smyrna Beach on Saturdays and Sundays almost every weekend. It cost $1.00 to drive your car on the beach, so we drove to the south end outside the city limits to avoid the toll. Today, the city charges $33 a day.

As college kids flocked to New Smyrna for its wide, automobile-drivable beach, we searched for a quieter stretch of sand to go to. The hardcore surfers at school raved about Cocoa Beach, but street parking was limited. We ventured straight east to Cocoa Beach for the rest of our college years, having no idea I would join the Air Force and my first assignment would be at the base where we spent so much time on its beach.

After high school, I attended Valencia Community College because I didn't get accepted to any state universities, and it was all I could afford at $3.00 a semester hour. I dreamed of becoming an artist since I was in elementary school. But after only two semesters in the art program, I realized I would starve in this profession. I switched to engineering to increase my probability of solid long-term employment with a pension. It was another good choice, but the degree required me to take eighteen+ credit hours a semester to stay on schedule.

In parallel with attending Valencia, I started work at United Parcel Service (UPS), loading trucks from 10:00 p.m. to 2:00 a.m., Monday through Friday. Suzanne's brother, Steve, worked there and put in a good word with the boss for me. UPS got its money's worth and paid me well, including full benefits, thanks to my Teamsters Union membership. Viet Nam veterans going to college on the GI Bill worked with me. Their stories were horrific, and they told us we were lucky to be living in the United States. I developed a deep respect for these young men I worked with.

Meanwhile, Suzanne and I dated throughout college, and she was my cheerleader, showing me a level of kindness I had not experienced in my life.

In the Easter season of 1978, we attended a sunrise service at SeaWorld. Arriving before sunrise, we found seats high in the amphitheater where Shamu the whale performed. The small stadium was almost filled to capacity. As the sun began to rise, the music began. The preacher, Brother Jim, explained that Jesus was indeed real using historical references.

In my mind, I always believed in God somehow. My earliest recollection was that at six years old, I read the book of Revelation because a friend said it explained the "end of the world." I didn't understand it, but it scared me, and I knew then I needed God in my life.

At the end of Pastor Jim's message, he asked the crowd who wanted to accept Jesus as their savior and ask for forgiveness of sins. As he prayed, he requested those people to raise their hands. I initially felt embarrassed in the crowd, but slowly I raised my left hand. As my outstretched hand rose, I felt like it was reaching to heaven.

On the drive home, I told Suzanne. She began to cry, believing I would change, and we would break up. I suggested the opposite, and she agreed to attend services at First Baptist in downtown Orlando.

Two weeks later, on a Sunday evening, our pastor offered an invitation to accept Jesus and come forward for prayer. Without hesitation, Suzanne silently left the pew and walked forward, with tears in her eyes. I can still her walking down the main aisle of the church.

Accepting Jesus as our Savior was the best choice we each would ever make in our lives. I'll never forget seeing her walk the aisle to answer the altar call. Who could have guessed we would both walk the same aisle two years later to be married? Jesus saved us for eternity that Easter and started changing our earthly lives for the better going forward. Two months later, we both were baptized at First Baptist.

We wore white robes provided by the staff as we waited nervously for our turn. I went first and turned to wait for Suzanne. Her face was bright with a huge smile as the pastor pulled her out of the water. Another day I will never forget.

Soon, I received my AA degree from Valencia and was accepted by Florida Tech—now University of Central Florida—because they had to accept community college transfers in Florida. Soon, I was led to join the military after watching all the Vietnam news and working with all the veterans at UPS. The only ROTC program on campus was with the Air Force, so I found their office and applied. I didn't tell my parents until after the deal was done, and Suzanne was fully supportive of this decision. The Air Force, desperate for recruits in the post-Vietnam environment, agreed to start the process since I was in good health and didn't have a prison record. But before the Air Force would accept me into the ROTC program, I was required to complete boot camp in California in August of 1978.

On a humid July morning my mother dropped me off at the small, nearly vacant, Orlando Airport. The airline stapled a luggage tag on my bag with MCO-SMF for my departure and arrival airports. The locals knew MCO stood for McCoy Air Force Base, which preceded the civilian airport. In 1958, the Pine Castle Air Force Base was renamed the McCoy Air Force Base in honor of General McCoy, who steered a B-47 with catastrophic engine failure away from an elementary school so it would crash in the surrounding pine trees. Everyone onboard died but the children in the school were safe.

Back to my flight, this was my first time on an airplane, which almost crashed into another plane when it attempted to land in Atlanta. To save money, the Air Force booked me on 5 flights on 5 different airlines for a 12-hour trip, not that the drill instructor cared when I arrived.

During the first mail call, I was the only one to get a card. The drill instructor sneered as he handed me the card. I received a card, sometimes more, every single day from Suzanne and was able to write her a few letters back at night under a wool blanket with a flashlight.

After a couple of weeks, when the drill instructor yelled "mail call," everyone looked at me. When he called my name, they all cheered.

About five weeks later, he yelled, "Carrick, this woman's in love. You gonna marry her?" Everyone laughed, but me. After I returned to Orlando, the Air Force forwarded me a few of her cards that had arrived after I flew home.

I completed boot camp and joined the Air Force ROTC Detachment 159, then registered for classes. I needed three more years of classes to complete my engineering degree, but the Air Force required me to complete the ROTC program in two years. So, based on a suggestion from one of the officers assigned to Detachment 159, I switched from engineering to computer science, having no idea what it was. But it was "science," and I could finish in 2 years if I took 21 hours a semester and attended all the summer semesters.

When I started the fall semester in 1978, Captain White took me under his wing. He was a C-130 pilot and a devout Christian who became one of the most influential people in my young life. I know Jesus put him and me in the same place for a good reason.

As my walk with Jesus continued, my perspective on life changed. I gained more discernment and viewed life more seriously. Soon, I realized I was in love with Suzanne. I talked to Captain White about it, and we prayed about it. A few weeks later, I asked her to marry me.

"I may never have much money, but I will always love you, and I promise we will always have fun."

In classic Suzanne style, she said, "Well, it's about time! I knew six months ago."

Then she paused, smiled, looked into my eyes, and said, "Yeah, let's go, Lee."

We officially made our second most important life choice. My family told me often that we would never make it together, and that the relationship would end soon in heartbreak. They did everything possible to break us up; the song "Some Say" by Rascal Flatts tells a similar story, but we moved forward in our engagement.

As I neared graduation and my commissioning, the Air Force pretended to give me a choice of locations for my first assignment. I filled out my Form 90, affectionately called the "Dream Sheet," adding New Mexico, California, and anywhere overseas as my preferences. I just wanted to get as far away from Orlando as possible.

Months passed. Finally, the phone rang in the cadet barracks. I grabbed the receiver.

"ROTC barracks, Cadet Carrick speaking."

"Carrick, get your butt to the Commandant's office. You got orders; you're going overseas!"

I literally ran across campus and burst into the Master Sergeant's room.

This well-worn Vietnam veteran laughed out loud, saying, "Yep, son, you're going overseas, over two causeways to Patrick Air Force Base."

My elation popped like a balloon. Patrick was forty-five miles east of Orlando, where Suzanne and I spent most of our weekends on the beach. I sulked out of the office; at least I received a location near an ocean.

Two months later, I graduated from college, accepted my commission in the Air Force, planned a wedding, and rented an apartment on the beach in Cape Canaveral.

Suzanne quit her full-time job working for an investment banker in downtown Orlando. She gave stability and calmness to our relationship, and I never would have finished college if not for Suzanne. Finally, our wedding would occur, much sooner than expected, and we could live the life we wanted.

THREE
Foundations

Planning and funding our wedding on a small budget resulted in the best outcome for us as a young couple. Instead of planning an expensive destination wedding and honeymoon, we planned our wedding more modestly. Our focus was on our future, not extravagant wedding and honeymoon events. The guidelines for marriage came from two one-hour premarital counseling sessions with the associate pastor at our church. Sermons on Ephesians and marriage books were our main source of information after that. In addition, my best man, Captain White, and his wife, Sharyn, taught us about marriage from a biblical perspective many Sunday afternoons at their home. The time they invested in us was the most impactful teaching to prepare us for marriage and happiness together. We chose to put Jesus first and made Him part of our daily life.

Destination weddings in 1980 meant guests hopped on the interstate and drove to the "destination." Our guests ventured to downtown Orlando to our home church, First Baptist Church. The red-brick building with white columns at the entrance stood among other large churches and city buildings, the best place to start our marriage.

We adopted traditional biblical roles for our marriage, ignoring the current cultural trends of our generation. The Bible never changes; its truths are eternal. I accepted full responsibility as the leader of our marriage, knowing I was accountable first to God in this role. It was a commitment I made to Jesus first, and to Suzanne second. The Bible provides clear guidelines for a husband, and I followed them as consistently as possible. In order for us to thrive as a couple, I needed to provide financial, physical, spiritual, and emotional security for her. Knowing she could trust me in all situations was paramount, and I made sure my actions were predictable and effective. I always tried to be "velvet steel" for her—strong in all situations, while maintaining a smooth and comfortable demeanor.

It was also my responsibility to maintain objectivity in our relationship. We always made decisions together, but when we were deadlocked, Suzanne asked me to break the impasse and make the best decision for both of us. The few times that happened, a heavy weight settled on me to ensure it was the right decision.

From the start, we made a conscious choice to support each other and appreciate our differences. Both of us were unique individuals with different life experiences and perspectives. However, we did not want to be independent; we knew that would lead us apart, and that was a nonstarter for us. Dependence required operating from a position of weakness for both of us, so we wanted to help each other grow individually and thus grow our married life. We chose interdependence, as it allowed us to retain our unique personalities and leverage our strengths to help each other, often to offset our individual weaknesses. It positioned us to care for each other and also hold each other accountable.

As we discussed what we wanted in our marriage, we unknowingly built common goals for us to pursue together that became a foundation for the longevity of our relationship. Even the simple standard wedding vows we exchanged established guidelines we would live by in life. The Bible was the core of our worldview, and Jesus gave us constant hope for the future. We learned that self-sacrifice was crucial to a solid, long-term marriage, and our vows needed to be promises to each other we would keep until death separated us.

As we began to implement these concepts in our relationship before we were married, we created a unique environment we wanted to live in together. It no longer mattered what our friends were doing; we decided what was best for us. This attitude changed the people we associated with, what we listened to, and reshaped our activities.

We lived in a time before social media created unrealistic expectations for young people by displaying new luxury cars, beautiful swimming pools, magnificent homes, and exotic trips as the path to happiness and debt. We realized our income level had nothing to do with our happiness, and this was foundational to building the conditions we would thrive in for more than forty-two years.

Our protective environment was similar to a bubble where we could be completely vulnerable inside and discuss any topic, speak what was in our hearts, and address fears and anxieties. I wanted Suzanne to thrive inside our bubble, but I never wanted to control her. She could become the woman she wanted to be, and, most importantly, she could become the woman that God envisioned her to be. It's always better to focus on someone other than yourself.

The wedding day arrived, and we did it all, setting a precedent for the rest of our marriage. Suzanne would always remark, "Do what we gotta do!"

No meal was provided due to our budget, and the church did not allow dancing or booze, so we saved lots of money. Before noon, we crafted tiny pimento cheese sandwiches and cheese crackers. Pickles were placed neatly on white ceramic trays, along with radish roses, which I was exceptionally good at making. All the reception treats were packed tightly in worn, opaque Tupperware containers courtesy of Suzanne's mother's job. The hatchback of my turquoise 1977 Buick Skyhawk overflowed.

We drove downtown and delivered it to the church wedding planner, who helped these two lone kids in love pull it off. Suzanne's friend's mother delivered beautiful flowers, worth much more than we paid her. I can still see Suzanne's expression as the flowers flowed into the church and were placed on the pews and altar. Her bouquet was hidden in a white plastic bag that made me realize this was for real.

Suzanne did her own hair and makeup and never complained about doing this. I met my best man, Captain White, at the church, and we changed into our 1970s velvet-lined tuxedos with wide lapels. I got dressed quickly and was in the church greeting guests afterward. I was elated, realizing that our lives were about to begin, as a constant smile revealed my happiness.

Soon, Captain White whisked me away from the crowd when the organ music started playing. Music filled the church at 7:00 p.m. on Tuesday, September 23, 1980, because my active duty would start six weeks early, and it was the only day our pastor was available.

I will always remember Suzanne's sparkling eyes and wide smile. In a deep Tennessee accent, Pastor Jim Henry led the service, but I only remember the vows and the altar call afterward, a Southern Baptist tradition. Talking with guests after the ceremony was bittersweet, as it would be the last time to see most of them before my active duty with the Air Force started. Suddenly, I was driving my bride in the Skyhawk to Captiva Island to start our new life together.

Captiva is a stunningly beautiful small tropical island on the west coast of Florida. Her brother owned a new condo there and kindly let us use it for our honeymoon for free. We spent hours walking on the long, white sandy beaches and collecting seashells. The peace of that honeymoon was a welcome change after the busy past six months.

However, on the third day, the clutch cable on my car snapped while driving in the condo complex. Fortunately, a maintenance worker helped me crawl under the car and complete the repair. None of this bothered Suzanne as she simply said she'd be at the pool unless I needed her help. Undaunted by the unexpected car repair expenses, I spent the huge sum of $25 each for a seafood buffet at the fanciest restaurant (there were only two) on Captiva to wrap up our honeymoon celebration.

After our honeymoon, we attended church services at First Baptist Orlando. I sat there so happy, rolling my wedding band around my finger to make sure it was real. Pastor Jim started a series on "The Family," speaking about biblical responsibilities of a husband. I thought he was talking only to me because it was about being a godly husband.

The next weekend, he focused on wives and then raising a family. Suzanne and I could not get enough of this teaching. We also learned more on these topics from cassette tapes (before the Internet, YouTube, and podcasts) from Dr. James Dobson and *Focus on the Family*.

The fact that I made little money in the Air Force was a blessing because it forced us to live a simple life. We often joked that our dates were grocery-shopping at the commissary, mowing the grass, pedaling our bikes, and riding in the car talking and enjoying the scenery. We couldn't afford fancy trips to exotic islands, and if the destination wasn't on I-95, we usually weren't going.

For years, people would ask me, "What makes you so happy? Why are you always smiling?"

I would simply reply, "My wife Suzanne. You'll understand once you get to know her."

* * *

Now that we were "man and wife," it was time to make the forty-five-mile trek to Cape Canaveral, Florida. We rented a large U-Haul truck, having no idea what size we needed for our sparse belongings. After we loaded the truck, we laughed because we had filled only twenty percent of its capacity. I started the tired truck, and we bounced along Highway 50 to the Treasure Beach Apartments in Cape Canaveral.

The sun had faded the poured concrete apartment building, which housed twelve furnished apartments with jalousie windows. Moving our limited belongings into the well-worn furnished apartment, I immediately noticed the two twin beds. Since you "do what you gotta do," I tied them together to make our first king-size bed, and we made the best of it. Most nights, I woke with my numb arm stuck between the mattresses.

Every morning, we drank coffee and watched the ocean waves crash against the white sand. Every afternoon when I returned home from work, we sat on the beach as the sun set. We were finally together, and life was glorious.

A couple of days later after we arrived, I reported for duty at 0700 at Patrick Air Force Base. After a couple of hours of signing papers, the sergeant directed me to the 6555 Aerospace Test Group at Kennedy Space Center, twenty miles north. Three months later, Suzanne landed a job with the McDonnell Douglas Company, working on a contract to prepare and install the satellites in the space shuttle.

We drove to work together engaging in lively discussion on our one-hour commute. Fortunately, my small sports car lacked a back seat, so we didn't have to carpool anyone else.

After dropping Suzanne off at the NASA Operations and Checkout Building early every morning, I headed to the NASA Vehicle Assembly Building by Launch Pad 36A. My role was in NASA Vehicle Engineering, a group responsible for configuring, testing, and launching the shuttle. Seeing spaceships, rockets, and satellites every day was surreal at times for both of us. It was also the first time I ever saw a computer, and there were hundreds used to launch the space shuttle. NASA was twenty years ahead of commercial industry.

A few months after moving into Treasure Beach, the Air Force notified me that a spacious 1950s three-bedroom, two-bath duplex with a garage was available. We jumped on the opportunity, and the nice older couple running Treasure Beach let us out of the lease with a smile and a wink at Suzanne, knowing she was a new bride with a military husband, and change would be often for her.

We quickly covered the concrete floors in our on-base house with well-worn, abused-by-many, wall-to-wall shag carpeting from a friend who was leaving base housing. Handing him a check for $125, we dragged the rug material room by room across the street to my house. No padding, only used carpet tape, and it fit perfectly.

We had a private communication system. Immediately, the smile on her face would transfer to mine. Best of all, we could just smile at each other and, without speaking a word, communicate volumes of love.

A year later, we sold our carpet for $125 and dragged it to the other end of the street to its next new home. For us, we had purchased our first house for $47,000 in Titusville,

Florida. My hand shook as I signed the mortgage with excitement and dread; after signing my life away, we drove to our new home. I carried Suzanne across the threshold, and soon we painted or wallpapered every room in the house.

Always joyful and grateful, she saw the bright side and avoided negative people. She was a quiet girl until she laughed. And when she did, you just had to join in. She loved the Word of God because it was always about hope, joy, and peace. There were challenges in life, but God was always there and always a place for redemption for us.

After settling into our new home, we joined Park Avenue Baptist Church, and a young married small group led by Rick and Barb that was foundational in our early marriage years. We loved living and working together, as our life remained simple, easy to do on a lieutenant's salary.

Working in a unique environment that was also distant from our hometown allowed us to build our own life and routine together. From the start, we were implementing the "cleave and leave" mindset, as described in Genesis 2:24; for us, it was more like "cling and sing." Both sets of parents were free with their criticisms, but their external negativity was deflected by our bubble. As the husband responsible for leading our marriage relationship, I addressed intrusive, disparaging comments diplomatically—honor thy father and mother, after all—but I wanted them to know there were limits to their statements. I told them where we stood, what was acceptable, and what was not. They typically didn't respond well, but I knew I had to stand my ground for my wife and marriage. And as long as our bubble was intact, it didn't really matter to us.

Suzanne accepted all people, and regardless of how long or short you knew her, she made you feel special. She connected with people quickly on a personal level and deeply cared. This was a unique trait of hers, and it drew people to her.

We had been married for about three years when Suzanne told me it was time to start a family. I knew what it took to get her pregnant and volunteered quickly. Soon, our son Matt was born at Wuesthoff Hospital in Rockledge, Florida. Suzanne was elated, as she always wanted to be mother, and we didn't know it was a boy until he was born. How times have changed. She loved that role and often said it's what she always wanted to be in life. Suzanne quit her job when Matt was born and never went back to work, the third best choice we ever made.

The Space Shuttle program soon expanded, and the Air Force planned to use it to launch reconnaissance satellites from Central California. With this change, they reassigned me to the 6595th Shuttle Test Group at Vandenberg AFB on the central coast of California.

I purchased the expensive $25 AAA membership, which gave us a dozen highway maps, the only way to get around before GPS and cellphones. To help, at the local AAA office, a nice lady opened a huge map of the entire United States and used a highlighter to mark every highway from Titusville, Florida, to Vandenberg AFB, California.

A few days later, the movers packed everything we owned into cardboard boxes and partially filled the empty moving trailer. Seeing everything we owned on a truck driving across the broken asphalt road headed west was an odd sensation. We had never seen everything we owned in one place rolling away from us. The next day, Suzanne and I packed our Pontiac Phoenix, which I purchased from her brother, tight for the three-week drive to California. Taking the southern route on I-10 provided better driving conditions, since it was February of 1985. No cellphones or

Internet, so we trusted all the maps and rolled along the road singing kid songs on Matt's portable cassette player. It was heaven, the three of us on a cross-country escapade in our bubble.

The next three years in California were formative for our marriage and may have been when we truly solidified the foundation of our relationship. We were forced to meet new people in a new land and join a new church. And we did it all on our own, as we clung to each other and took risks figuring it all out.

Our military family was better than our own, and we loved living there making many long-term friends. I also was blessed with a top-notch boss, Lt Col Rich Niederhauser, who set the example, led with integrity, and defended his troops well. He helped shape my leadership style also. His wife, Sandra, looked out for the wives, and Suzanne loved her.

Soon, Suzanne knew it was time to add to our family, and you know my response. On a typical foggy morning in September 1986, at Vandenberg AFB on the central coast of California, Betsy joined the family. Suzanne was thrilled to have a girl. Betsy's closet overflowed with pretty dresses and hair bows, and she had plenty of stuffed animals on her bed. Suzanne always thought it was interesting that her kids were born on both coasts, about 2,800 miles apart. "Guess we didn't see that one coming," she would say.

The Air Force offered me an assignment to a remote office in Washington, DC, in 1988. After discussing the options and praying with Suzanne about it, we agreed to move again. With two young kids and limited funds, we decided it would be best for me to buy a house while on one of my temporary duty trips to Virginia. This was still before our current technology, so I called Suzanne from a payphone and tried to describe the houses and neighborhoods. She listened attentively, asked a couple of questions, and then would say, "Lee, I trust you. You'll make a good decision for us."

I selected a 1,000-square-foot house with a partially finished basement. I knew I could convert the unfinished basement into two more bedrooms and a laundry room. It also did not have a garage, which was no fun when it snowed. I was the only guy in the squadron who didn't have a garage. The house was all I could afford, but it would become a good home because what really mattered was what occurred on the inside, memories with my family. I thought it was absolutely crazy to buy a house solo, but Suzanne said she trusted me, and it would be fine.

When I returned home from Virginia on these temporary trips, I had my photographs developed and anxiously showed the house I bought for our family to Suzanne. She smiled. "It's a lovely house; you did good, Lee." I realized again what an amazing woman I married.

I hoped the old Pontiac could make the 2,800-mile trip to Virginia. To be extra sure, I had a new transmission installed in the car due to its high mileage.

Once again, the moving truck carried all our possessions down the road enroute to northern Virginia. Early the next morning, we loaded the kids, said a prayer, and started rolling. About two hours south, the new transmission blew a seal. We got a tow and spent the night in a dirty motel next to the AAMCO transmission store.

The next day, we drove from Palm Springs to Phoenix. It was so hot, the car would overheat when I used the air conditioning. At 110 degrees, it was cooler to drive with the windows closed without the air-conditioning. We took turns driving across the desert and wiping the kids with cold towels to keep them cool. It was so hot, their crayons melted in their containers. We had no choice but to keep going, as there were no motels along the desert road. Once we arrived in Phoenix, we quickly got the kids into the hotel swimming pool.

When we arrived in Manassas, Virginia, we turned onto the street to our new house, the one Suzanne had never seen. As we pulled onto the sloped asphalt driveway, she viewed the aluminum-sided split foyer with a brick chimney. She smiled as she looked at me and said it was a great house. If she didn't like the house or neighborhood, she never mentioned it. Of course, I carried her across the threshold after we put the kids inside their playpen.

My new job was with Air Force Special Projects to build, deploy, and operate systems for the National Reconnaissance Office, which at that time was highly classified. The group I worked with was a small band of young guys completely focused on the mission. It would become one of the best jobs I would ever have, mostly due to the people I worked with. My boss, Dennis Adams, was an awesome leader, and I still stay in touch with my coworkers Kevin Keating, Sid Fuchs, and Scot Shier after almost forty years later. Our team bonded quickly, while our wives and families became close friends as well.

I traveled frequently for my work but tried to limit trips as much as possible. Because of this, I had the fewest flight miles of anyone in my group, while my boss hit the 1,000,000 miles flown club with United Airlines (UA). When I did travel, I took late departure flights and red-eye flights home to be with Suzanne and the kids.

While I was traveling and working, Suzanne ran our home and family effectively. She had two young children and a home to manage, but she never once complained. Both kids walked to George C. Round Elementary School with their friends in our neighborhood. Based on her love of baseball, Suzanne enrolled Matt in T-ball. A dance demonstration at school captivated Betsy, and she quickly joined the Prince William County Recreation dance company. We were so happy together in our bubble.

Four years later in 1992, my next assignment was at the Pentagon, which was a great and bad job at the same time. The work pace was insane, and everyone I knew was on the verge of burnout. We kept an empty milk jug under our desks in case the men's room was unavailable. It also required me to leave the house in the dark to catch a commuter bus or van and return later that evening, still in the dark. The Pentagon had not changed much in fifty years. My boss's office had one wall covered with a map of Germany, with markings for bombing raids and attacks from World War II. The windows didn't close, and it was really cold in the winter.

There were vents for heat from the basement, five floors down, but there were so many rats in the building that we had to cover the vents every night. Summers were worse, as the air conditioning was weak and still had those windows that didn't close completely. The Pentagon looked and smelled like a prison, but it was likely in worse condition.

One of the bright spots was my boss, Lt Col John O'Connor, a self-described Strategic Air Command "Trained Killer" in the USAF Nuclear Missileer career field. He overlooked my lack of knowledge and brought me into the fold. I appreciated his hard work ethic, attention to detail, commitment to the thankless mission and ability to laugh no matter how hard and crazy it got, almost every day, in the five-sided building.

Suzanne maintained control at home and always smiled to welcome me when I returned home; this was a blessing to me that could not be matched. To greet her with a hug and a kiss, then for the kids to run up and greet me was the best part of every day. She made everything pleasant, never complaining about my long hours at work. It helped that she believed in the mission I was working on as well. We offset my extensive work schedule by filling the weekends with family time and church on Sundays. Playing kickball in the backyard or roller skating in the neighborhood was far better than long hours and high stress in the Pentagon.

Suzanne made everything in my life beautiful. There was always a warmth throughout our home when she was there. She effortlessly changed my life for the better and was the only person to truly love me. And to me, she was the most beautiful woman I had ever seen. Her gorgeous blue-green eyes shimmered in the sunlight. Beneath her captivating gaze, she always had a smile. Usually a wide check-to-cheek smile, just shy of breaking into laughter.

Despite the hectic lifestyle, Suzanne and I focused on treating each other with respect. In the Bible, the book of James 2:20 states, “You foolish person, do you want evidence that faith without deeds is useless?” We applied the same principle to love in ordinary daily tasks and the everyday words we spoke over each other, living out the truth of faith with deeds. The challenge would be to avoid, or at least manage, the constant distractions and temptations of day-to-day life with jobs and children. Some ways we did this was through avoiding harsh words and treating each other with deep respect. The consistent appreciation for each other made our marriage stronger.

For years, when I met new people, they asked what hobbies I had. I would reply with, “My wife Suzanne.” Why spend hours on a golf course when I could be with her instead? Most folks thought I was crazy, but I knew the truth.

In 1995, I retired from the Air Force and joined a small company, TASC, that provided services and products to the National Reconnaissance Office. Travel was always necessary, and I hated to be away from Suzanne. To help, I kept a couple of small photos of her and the kids in my wallet for long flights to remind myself of why I was doing this.

When Apple released the iPod, I bought one and added songs that reminded me of my time with Suzanne. I updated the Suzanne playlist regularly, but the top ten rarely changed. "I Was Made to Love Her" tells our story and how nothing would ever stop me from loving her. Later versions of the iPod would also store many photographs. I listened to the playlist and viewed the pictures whenever I was away, but the music and images could be streamed in my mind without the iPod. Those images of her and our favorite songs remain locked in my heart to this day.

Rank	**Lee's "Suzanne Playlist" Top Ten**	**Artist**
1	*"True Believers"*	Darius Rucker
2	*"I Was Made to Love Her"*	Stevie Wonder
3	*"Want To"*	Sugarland
4	*"What's Going On"*	Marvin Gaye
5	*"Some Say"*	Rascal Flatts
6	*"Wouldn't It Be Nice"*	The Beach Boys
7	*"Unforgettable"*	Nat King Cole
8	*"Sunshine of My Life"*	Stevie Wonder
9	*"Overjoyed"*	Stevie Wonder
10	*"That Girl"*	Stevie Wonder

In 2002, Matt graduated from high school and had been accepted to George Mason University in Fairfax, Virginia, leaving Suzanne both overjoyed and heartbroken. We were excited as we moved his belongings into the dorm and managed to hold back the tears until we drove home.

Two years later, we repeated the process, dropping Betsy off at George Mason. Suzanne was so proud of both, but the early days as empty nesters were not fun for either of us. However, in a few months, we realized we were a couple again. Suddenly, we were like newlyweds, and we quickly transitioned into this wonderful new life together. Did we miss the kids? Sure. Did we want them back, living with us full-time? No way!

She was always a silly girl, full of laughter and play. We had the best time with simple things in life, playing many unspoken games with unknown rules full of mystery and fun through the years.

This new freedom was exhilarating, and we had a blast. We could do whatever we wanted, go anywhere, eat anything, buy anything, say everything out loud, wear what we liked, or wear nothing at all. Initially guilt-ridden for having so much fun, we quickly dumped those foolish thoughts and enjoyed this new life together. Suzanne and I always heard how terrible being an empty nester was; for us, the change provided amazing times, and as long as we were together, life was good. Thankfully, my job was only for employment and never more important than our marriage.

A larger company bought the small company I worked for, which was soon bought by an even larger company. The increased bureaucracy led me to seek a new job, and Ross Perot hired me to lead his US federal government business line. Susan Nolan, our CIO, was a solid Christian and gave me a book to read—*Halftime: Moving from Success to Significance* by Bob Buford in 1994. The book's premise is that at the midpoint of one's life, consider switching from "success to significance." Everyone needed to work toward "success" to pay off the mortgage, put the kids through college, and save for retirement.

Once those core responsibilities were completed, shift one's attention to helping other people and serving the Lord, focusing on "significance." This mindset changed my perspective dramatically.

A few years later, Ross Perot sold his company to Michael Dell, CEO of Dell Computers. I returned to the intelligence sector for a less demanding job, which required me to swallow my ego and not seek a leadership role; it turned out to be a good choice and made it easier to transition to retirement. During this time, Suzanne built a relationship with Tonia at USO Headquarters in DC. Suzanne began helping Frank, the USO lead at Shindand Air Base in northern Afghanistan. Soon, whenever Frank needed anything for the troops, he contacted Suzanne and she began shipping boxes of supplies. Several years later, the USO told me they adopted Suzanne's process for training and supporting deployed USO members around the world.

As I approached fifty-five, Suzanne recalled a dinner we had with a coworker and his wife ten years prior. They were about to retire and told us they should have begun planning for their retirement much earlier. He recommended we start planning for our retirement when we hit fifty-five. Again, Suzanne was the deep thinker with perspective in our marriage and felt this approach was important.

We didn't want to leave the kids behind in Virginia but knew we eventually needed to move south to a smaller, warmer town near the beach and a military base for us to use its services as retirees. This also meant it would be a conservative town with good churches. We agreed it didn't make sense to make decisions based on the kids, as they would not make living decisions based on where we lived, so we decided to move south. We prayed about this decision often and knew it was the right one.

Suzanne suggested we vacation in cities that were candidates for our retirement, and her wisdom and insights were always spot on. We enjoyed searching through maps of the cities on the coasts from Virginia to Florida.

One day after dinner, Suzanne said, with a huge smile, "How about Charleston?"

"South Carolina?" I snarled. "That little state? It's got nothing. Why would anyone live there?"

Unfazed by my usual lack of perspective and knowledge, she displayed photos and facts about the area. We had not been there, but it checked all the items on our priority list. My common sense finally took hold, and I thought, *Trust her, Lee; she's never wrong.*

In 2012, she planned a trip to Charleston for our wedding anniversary. We stayed in a hotel that had been the original Citadel, on Marion Square. I still remember walking the streets with her in awe, as we knew almost instantly this would be our new hometown. People were friendly, and the area was beautiful. The atmosphere was similar to growing up in Florida, but instead of the entertainment culture Orlando had, Charleston had a rich history.

After six more trips over the following year, we started the search for a home. She really liked a house in Charleston, South Carolina, but said it wasn't the time; it was too early. I was willing to buy it despite it being a fixer-upper. She said we should wait.

The realtor called three months later, stating the owners had dropped the price again, and it wouldn't last long. I told Suzanne, and with tears in her eyes, she admitted she loved that house and had been praying every night that it would be ours. The owners accepted our offer the next day.

Moving to Charleston was another great choice of ours, which was based on Suzanne's insights. She loved Charleston, no regrets. After living there for a couple of years, we understood why it's called the "Holy City" —so many great churches there. Suzanne told me a couple of years before she realized Jesus led us to Charleston specifically to attend Seacoast Church and was glad our two kids soon followed us after graduating school. They both had accepted Christ as their Savior years ago and liked the church. Suzanne loved Seacoast, another choice that made a huge difference in our lives, but I didn't know how important it would be to us until eight years later.

* * *

Throughout her life, Suzanne taught me that kindness was a strength, not a weakness. She knew the military protocols at formal events and understood how to roll with the corporate big-shots. Those events bored her, but she did them for me, anyway. She enjoyed real people as well, on a first-name basis with our mailman, our UPS driver, the recycling man, the refuse man, and many others. Suzanne provided cold Gatorade for them in the summer and Christmas gifts in the winter. When we rode our bikes around the neighborhood, the big trucks would pass by with a honk and wave. She loved it.

Suzanne said, "These are the important people that keep this great country running; they never get the credit they are due. But Jesus understands; He knows."

She was also a woman of action, tough as nails. Focused on fitness, she was proud to be at her high school weight (well, maybe plus five), never took prescription medication, vaccines, and rarely even had an aspirin. She exercised regularly, and we rode bicycles fifteen-plus miles daily when we were in our sixties

***

At a men's worship night at Seacoast, the men's pastor introduced a lady from Kids Coast, the children's ministry, to me. She sought male volunteers, as it was important for the kids to see men serving in the children's ministry. Her offering was on my mind every day for two weeks. I knew nothing about babies and young kids, but I thought I could at least fix things or paint a wall. Thankfully, deciding to volunteer was another good choice for me.

The first day I volunteered, the Kidscoast lead, picked a coffee cup at random and handed it to me without looking at it. "Here ya go!" she said with a big smile.

I chuckled, then I read the words on the front: *Let The Adventure Begin.* I showed her the mug's statement.

"Well, whadda you know about that!" she said, and we laughed at the irony. Neither of us knew what that meant, but I would soon find out because there are no coincidences in God's kingdom.

Meanwhile, Matt worked for the federal government as a digital signal processing engineer in the Washington DC area for five years. His assigned projects supported important technologies and challenged him intellectually, but the downside was the hectic pace the work required. I had similar jobs in my past and knew what was required of him. After much prayer, he elected to leave government service and move to South Carolina in search of a new direction for his professional career. Suzanne encouraged him to live with us to get acquainted with the community first, and a friend from church helped him find a house a few months later.

The day after Matt moved out, Suzanne and I caught head colds. These colds hit us hard, and we were uncomfortable for three weeks, which was unusual for us. Trips to the doctor and the resulting antibiotics helped our conditions, but Suzanne's congestion continued to return. An X-ray revealed a small amount of pneumonia in her left lung. After a couple of rounds of increased antibiotics, her doctor scheduled a Computed Tomography (CT) scan by a specialist. If we only knew what was to come.

PART 2

SURVIVING

FOUR

Don't Get Mad at God
Wednesday, December 7th

Early Wednesday morning, Suzanne was awake when I woke up. Diminished lung capacity from the pneumonia slowed her actions. Her spirits were high, always positive, and she never complained, but she remained in the white chair in the corner of the bedroom for the day.

"Can you walk the dogs, please?"

It was difficult to hear her weak tone. Our miniature schnauzer and yorkie quivered, anticipating the ceramic sound of kibbles dropping into their bowls.

"Let's go to the emergency room now, Suzanne. Get the CT scan done earlier."

With a whisper, she declined and continued to hide her pain and fear, never wanting to concern me. Followed by the two anxious dogs, I retrieved their leashes from the pantry as tears filled my eyes. Something was wrong, very wrong, and I felt helpless for Suzanne.

After getting them fed, I cut fresh strawberries for Suzanne, adding blueberries and plain low-fat yogurt to her breakfast bowl. The clock advanced more slowly than usual, and my cellphone chiming interrupted washing dishes. It was a text from Bridget, the Kidscoast leader that Suzanne and I worked with at that time.

Bridget: You both are going to be
there tonight at 6:30? Right?

Lee: I'll be there after Suzanne's CT scan at 4:30, but I'll take her home first.

Bridget: OK.

That night at seven p.m., Seacoast Church's annual volunteer appreciation service would kick off; *The Polar Express* theme created a fun tone for the evening. Christmas trees, garland, and strings of lights would cast a happy glow throughout the church for the holiday season.

Finally, four p.m. arrived, and I drove Suzanne to the hospital for the scan. I stopped at the front door to shorten her walk and helped her to the outpatient area. The large and nearly empty waiting room provided many seating options. Few people were present, and most of the office doors were closed. After I checked her in at the nurse's desk, I sat next to Suzanne. Idle, meaningless chit-chat passed the time. My mind continued to race while Suzanne sat quietly, with no expression, atypical for her.

A call for "Suzanne Carrick" broke the silence as a small, demure nurse entered the waiting room carrying a clipboard under her arm. Suzanne stood cautiously and walked slowly behind the nurse back to the examination room; she seemed weaker by the hour. I sat silently, praying for answers and healing.

Twenty-two minutes passed when I heard, "Eugene Carrick." The same nurse's face was pale as she stared at me. "The doctor wants to see you," she explained.

Immediately, I sensed bad news. My mind raced faster, drowning out the hospital noise. Following the nurse close behind, the thought, *No matter what happens, I am not going to get mad at God,* crossed my mind. Was it my thought or a whisper from God? It didn't matter as I knew instinctively it was true, and I would need Jesus now more than ever. But why? Trusting Him, no matter what, was the only way, as my choice made in seconds would sustain me for what was to come. Our adventure was headed to my most dreaded event, the only one that I believed could cripple me for the rest of my life.

I turned the corner into the CT scan room; the doctor smiled through his full dark beard.

"Her lungs are a mess! She has a really bad case of pneumonia, and that's good news because we know how to treat that!"

I thought he was joking and cast my eyes to Suzanne, sitting on the CT scan machine.

"I was so worried," she exclaimed. "Now I know what it is!" Her eyes were bright, and she wore the biggest smile I had seen in weeks.

I was elated to have an answer and a path forward for her. The radiology doctor explained the next steps were testing to determine the cause, which could be bacteria, virus, or fungi. After a joyful embrace, Suzanne and I found a couple of chairs in the waiting room, holding hands tightly. I texted Bridget to let her know we would miss the service since Suzanne was admitted to the hospital for routine testing. No response suggested she was busy preparing for the service.

Doors soon swung open, and a nurse ushered us into an exam room to start the testing. Upstairs, an isolation room was prepared to ensure no new organisms entered Suzanne's lungs during the testing phase. Her nurse explained that the nurses would be wearing masks and asked if I wanted a mask.

"I'll pass, thank you."

This room would be temporary until the isolation room was ready. Pulling out a hospital gown, the nurse asked if I was her husband. I nodded yes as Suzanne slipped the soft, well-worn, flowered gown over her head and slid into the hospital bed with the nurse's assistance.

A petite female technician burst into the room; her bedside manner was already trained. The young nurse explained she was starting nursing school the next month at Trident Technical School in Charleston. Her mother and grandmother had paved her way into the family business in the nursing profession. I was struck by her maturity and commitment.

Where do these people come from? How do they dedicate their lives to helping people in such need? I wondered.

The young nurse said a technician would be in soon to start the blood tests as she left the room. I talked with Suzanne in the meantime, and we were both so glad it was only pneumonia. The room enveloped us in peace. I had lost track of time; my watch reported six-thirty p.m. The "Dream Team Appreciation Night" would start soon.

Pulling my cellphone from my pants pocket, I attempted to livestream the church service. But we had no connection to a cellular signal, and the app spun helplessly. I slid the useless cellphone back into my pocket and small-talked about the weekend to break the silence with Suzanne.

The sterile round clock on the wall showed nearly seven p.m. I attempted to livestream the service one more time but still had no connection.

Suddenly, the door burst open with a bang as a nurse technician pushed a large metal rolling cart full of vials and syringes into the room. She was in her forties, suggesting experience for the task at hand. Blood from Suzanne's arm was injected into each vial, allowing any present organisms to grow over the next 24 to 48 hours. After thirty minutes, the nurse completed her task. Glad she was done, I felt at ease knowing the doctors would soon discover the cure for Suzanne.

I remembered the Seacoast event again and tapped my cellphone in hopes that it would connect this time. Immediately, the live stream flowed smoothly, and we both watched as Bridget walked to the podium to speak.

Suzanne smiled. "That's great timing, Lee!"

We both loved Bridget's commitment to the ministry, positive attitude, and constant smile. She was an inspiration and one of the main reasons we enjoyed volunteering in Kids Coast. Bridget always went out of her way to thank us for our support. Her face was always bright and conveyed joy whenever she spoke.

She stepped to the podium and spoke to a large crowd of guests, volunteers, and staff members.

"Sometimes you get a gift you didn't know you needed. And Kids Coast got such a gift when these two volunteered. They prepared classrooms, copied and distributed the teaching material to all the rooms, cleaned the area, and ensured each work cart had plenty of tape, crayons, scissors, staplers, and children's Bibles."

She paused and looked at the crowd with a forced smile. "They also built things we needed. And most importantly, they made it all fun. They were always smiling. They drew cartoons and left messages for the staff. So, it's my pleasure to present the 'Love People' award to Suzanne and Lee Carrick. Unfortunately, they could not be here tonight."

After her statement, Bridget's face was grim as she stepped away from the podium; she conveyed a sense that something was wrong in her mannerisms. I wasn't sure; it's just seemed out of the ordinary.

Suzanne's eyes were wet with tears. "They gave us an award? Wow. We don't do that much. Bridget is awesome. All those girls are awesome."

Classic Suzanne, always engaged, quietly contributing. Constantly smiling, asking what more she could do to help. She never wanted to be in the spotlight, but she wanted to be in the game.

Watching the live presentation at church gave me a needed uplift to the bizarre day, unaware that the next five days would be more bizarre.

We fell silent after the award presentation, wishing we were at Seacoast with all the people instead of in the hospital room, with all the bright lights, medical equipment constantly beeping, and chemicals that filled the air with an antiseptic aroma. The last time Suzanne was in a hospital was when Betsy was born thirty-five years prior. Suzanne was never sick and rarely went to a doctor; her sixty-sixth birthday was only a month away.

I kept thinking that I wanted to take Suzanne home and leave all this behind, as this didn't feel right.

A few minutes passed, and an emergency room doctor entered the room and introduced himself. It always surprised us how young the doctors and nurses were, but maybe it was really because we were getting older. The doctor told Suzanne she would be there for a couple of days while they continued the blood tests. He added that the cultures take hours to grow, and for us to please understand it was a slow process.

"Because of the severity of your pneumonia, I am going to start you on a heavy-duty general antibiotic. It should help but won't be as effective as the one we'll use once we know the source of the infection." He paused in case we had questions; when we didn't, he continued speaking.

"Your oxygen saturation is a little low, so I am going to start you on some supplemental oxygen. That will help you breathe and make you feel better as well."

The doctor handed Suzanne a clear mask with a strap to hold in the mask place. He connected the thin, clear tube to an outlet in a green-colored plate on the wall labeled "OXYGEN." A digital display on a green plate displayed "2%" next to the label "ML." He smiled as he left the room.

My heart raced seeing Suzanne wearing an oxygen mask, my mind splitting between, "This is normal," and "This is a problem." Her history of excellent health clouded my understanding, as did my unwillingness to accept the gravity of the situation. I kept telling myself she would be fine and kept a smile on my face. Also, I knew she was in the best place possible.

It had been almost five hours since we left the house, so Suzanne asked me to go home and take the dogs out for a break. Before I left, I took a picture of her lying in her hospital bed. She gave me a huge smile and flashed her characteristic two-finger peace sign with her right hand. I'm not sure why I took that photo, but I am glad I did now. She was pretty in the well-worn, rumpled hospital gown. And her smile told me she was happy. I could see in her eyes that she loved me—only she could do that with a glance.

The dogs ignored me as I walked into the house, scampering behind me seeking Suzanne and running throughout the house with crazy zoomies. I could not get them to stop looking for her so I led them downstairs into our garage so they could check her car and see that it was empty. Everyone liked Suzanne, and I always knew why.

I took care of the dogs as quickly as possible and backed her car out of the garage. About thirty minutes had passed since I had to go home, and when I re-entered Suzanne's hospital room, there were doctors and nurses in her room. They were conducting more tests and talking, using a lot of Latin terms. The level of testing seemed extensive to me, but I didn't know the process.

I trusted the doctors and ignored the feeling of uncertainty as they worked for the next hour around her. Thankfully, I was pleasantly surprised by the genuine kindness the doctors and nurses showed her. It also helped that Suzanne showed her appreciation to every doctor and nurse who visited her.

The nurses apologized for the many painful blood draws they had to give her.

Suzanne smiled and said, "It needs to be done, and you're doing a great job, thank you." I could tell the nurses didn't expect that type of response.

As this testing progressed over the next hour, I realized she was building a partnership with the nurses. She initiated an important process that would help her from that point forward with her hospital care. By eleven at night, the doctors and nurses left.

Suzanne was tired by then, so I kissed her and drove home, feeling good that the doctors were working hard to help her recover from the pneumonia. And I knew they would identify the cause and send her home.

When I arrived home, I logged onto the hospital's webpage to review her blood tests. Reading her results, however, I realized the seriousness of her situation. The blood tests were all normal, except for immunoglobulin E (IgE) and tuberculosis. Something inside me started to crumble, as I had never been in this situation with Suzanne. She literally never was sick.

My mind raced with this news, and suddenly I broke down. I fell face-first on my bed, sobbing like I never had before in my life. My whole world was wrapped around Suzanne, and she was in the ICU, helpless. I cried out to God, begging Him to help her. And I heard inside my mind these precise and distinct words from a voice I knew was God's:

"I love her more than you do."

I'd never really thought about it before, but suddenly I knew it was true. Completely true.

"You have to let go of her."
"You have to trust Me."
"I will give her back to you."

I knew God was telling me He was in control. I said, "Yes, Lord," and immediately, my anxiety disappeared.

No more stress, no more tears. He was taking care of her, and I never questioned why. His words were so clear, and the peace I received was immediate.

FIVE

Isolation
Thursday, December 8th

I rolled over in bed, searching for my alarm clock: 7:01 appeared in a dull electronic glow that pierced my darkened bedroom. Instinctively, my hand searched for my cellphone hidden on the nightstand. The blue glow filled the room as I clicked on the text message app.

(Note: The only way we communicated for four days was via texting. I transcribed all text messages between Suzanne and I directly from her cellphone. Typographical and grammar errors were not corrected to maintain authenticity.)

Suz: I got moved to ICU a T 330 for the negative pressure room. Not much sleep. More blood work

Lee: ok

Suz: Not sure if they will let you come in this room. You'll have to ask

Lee: OK..how do you feel

Suz: Ok. tired. So much noise and beeping

Lee: it's always like that

Suz: More antibiotic at 4 am. They come and go through a side door.

Room air is being filtered for germs
I think. Not that I am critical

Lee: Ok

Suz: Ok gonna try to rest

The nurses moved her to the negative-pressure room in the ICU on the 2nd floor at 3:30 in the morning. Several blood tests and CT scans through the night prevented sleep for her.

Suz: so tired so much noise and
beeping

My heart broke as I never wanted her to suffer. Another test for tuberculosis was inconclusive, requiring her to remain in the isolation room with limited access. Doctors and nurses wore full-coverage biological protective gear with face shields to enter her room. It was a bizarre sight, but necessary to keep tuberculosis in the room and other harmful organisms out. This allowed them to test in a sterile environment to determine the cause of the pneumonia.

When I arrived at 8:03 a.m., the nurses walked me to her room. Light yellow curtains covered the double glass doors. Through a small 18x24 window, I saw Suzanne resting in the large hospital room; seeing her connected to the monitors and intravenous bag shocked me.

Lee: They said the doctor is making
rounds in 5 min and said to wait

Suz: Then you can come in?

Lee: Not sure

On my left, four doctors pushed a plastic two-level cart covered with machine printouts; two nurses followed close behind. None were smiling, and I assumed that's how it always is in the ICU. The team reviewed each patient's latest test results and decided on courses of action for the day. Suzanne's doctor stopped by Room #1 and motioned for me to join them and listen. More Latin terms were spoken as they perused the printed charts. The radiologist said he had uploaded her CT scan from a couple of hours ago.

A couple of hours ago? They sure are giving her a lot of tests.

"Why so many CT scans?" I asked the doctors.

They responded that it's typical for a lung infection. Their response didn't make sense to me, but I had no reason to not believe them.

The doctors gave Suzanne a generic antibiotic, Zyson, intravenously to slow the bacterial infection, and they wanted to see if it was slowing the growth of the pneumonia. They didn't offer to show me the CT scan, and I would find out why in a couple of days. Her doctor closed the laptop and summarized her status for me.

He said all the doctors, including the specialists, were surprised at how healthy Suzanne was, especially for her age of sixty-five. They commented that she was literally in perfect health, except for pneumonia, of course.

The older doctor asked again if she had traveled out of the country in the last month in the hopes of finding a reason for the possible tuberculosis.

"She hasn't been out of the *county* in the last month," I said.

They all laughed, and it helped break the tension. I could tell they were perplexed by her condition, so he asked again what prescriptions she had been on recently.

"Only the antibiotics a couple of weeks ago."

He shook his head and said he knew that fact and needed to know what she had been taking for the last four or five years.

"That's an easy question, Doc. She took an ibuprofen pill a few weeks ago."

More chuckles. "Not even any vaccinations?" he asked.

I shook my head.

He frowned, then said all her bloodwork came back normal, except the tuberculosis test, which was still neutral, adding he really doubted she had the disease but could not medically rule it out yet. I could tell her case was not making sense to them as they moved to Room #2.

Suz: What did they tell you

Lee: Nurse said pulmonary doc said you don't have TB

Suz: Ok

Lee: so they are all surprised how healthy you are. They keep asking what meds and illnesses you have and I keep saying none, they think it's basically pneumonia and they will keep giving you antibiotics. All your blood work has come back good. Doctor kept asking about the blood work and the nurses kept saying 'normal'

Suz: Good

Lee: GOD is in charge

Suz: Yes

> Lee: He [her doctor] isn't clearing you for TB yet. but I think they are being extra cautious for you and them. They want a phlegm sample today to figure out what the bacteria is

The team recommended more tests to include another CT scan. One nurse called for a technician to prep Suzanne and roll her bed to the exam room. She had to remain in a hospital bed because she required the constant flow of supplemental oxygen. I quickly texted her the doctors' comments.

She read her phone, looked at me, shrugged her shoulders, and smiled.

I told her all her vitals were good, and they were impressed by how healthy she was (as you see above).

After reading the text on her phone, she smiled and gave me a thumbs-up. A nurse and technician entered the small anteroom to don the extensive protective gear before moving into her room. Suzanne waved to me as they wheeled her to the elevator. She continued to wear the oxygen mask as they pushed her bed down the hall to the elevator. Still, nothing made sense to me.

A nurse left her station and offered a stool for me to sit on outside Suzanne's room in a narrow vestibule. After standing for a couple hours, it was a welcome relief, and I would need it for the rest of the day.

The morning was warm and sunny, and I decided to take a walk around the hospital while waiting for her. A flood of high school kids carrying instruments walked into the lobby. A sign announced the Wando High School Band would be performing a Christmas concert with classical music at nine-thirty a.m. The group was about half-female and half-male.

One girl wore bright pink hair and was getting her huge bass cello out of its case. Next to her, a tall, fit football-player-type guy was tuning his violin. They all dressed differently, were different heights, and had different ethnic backgrounds. Some were dressed nicely; others had on the same clothes they had probably slept in the night before.

But the amazing part is that this diverse group of kids all became one as they played music. Their love for music had unified them.

Their glorious music cascaded through the two-story lobby. Nurses, doctors, and visitors walked out of offices to listen and watch these talented young adults. Classical Christmas music and popular Christmas tunes filled the air.

The beauty of the music struck me, as these amazing people played and loved doing so. I reflected on the beauty of Christmas, not the decorations, but the birth of Christ. God sent love to earth in the form of man on that day in history. Love that would change the world forever. Love that would save mankind from death. Love that had changed Suzanne's life and mine over the last forty-eight years.

The beauty of Christmas music and the Christmas story brought tears to my eyes. I walked toward the stairs to the ICU on the second floor as the glorious music filled the large foyer.

I checked in at the ICU desk to see when Suzanne would return to her room; the nurse estimated two hours. I pulled my cellphone out of my left pants pocket to text Bridget.

Lee: Hey, can I pick up Suzanne's gift basket from the event last night?

Bridget: come on

I found Bridget in the church lobby when I arrived, smiling as usual. I gave her the highlights on Suzanne and said the doctors expect her to be home by the weekend. She appeared relieved and added that the Kids Coast team was praying for Suzanne's recovery. She handed me the gift basket and a certificate based on *The Polar Express*. It was the "Love People" award with an image of a Golden Ticket on the bottom that had the letters "B E L I E V E" written boldly across the front of the ticket. The word burned into my brain; I did believe in Jesus, and I believed Suzanne would be going home soon. I thanked Bridget and walked toward the exit, passing the chapel first before I would reach my car.

I felt led to pray for Suzanne in the church's chapel at that moment. It was old school because Jesus can hear our prayers wherever we talk to Him. Location doesn't matter to Jesus; what's in our hearts does.

I walked into the empty chapel. At the front was a wooden cross, like all the rooms in our church. Prayers pinned over the years had punctured hundreds of small holes into the dark wooden cross. As I stood and viewed the cross, so many thoughts ran through my mind. Most were about how much I loved Suzanne and all the fun we had together. Now my best friend was in the ICU, and doctors were uncertain of her condition.

I kneeled next to the cross and prayed Jesus would heal her, either through the doctors or through Jesus' healing power. Immediately, I heard God's voice speaking to my mind in a soft whisper this time:

"I love her more than you do. You have to let go of her and trust Me. I will give her back to you."

I was stunned; God had given me the same exact message last night. I agreed again with God's request.

I saw a friend while I was there, who suggested I start keeping a journal. Although it seemed like an odd request, I decided to stop at Wal-Mart on the way back to see Suzanne. I purchased three college-ruled spiral bound notebooks and pens and drove to the hospital.

As the automatic ICU doors slowly opened at 3:30 p.m., I quietly walked in, checking Room #1 on the right side of the hall. Suzanne saw me and waved from behind the glass doors. I was relieved to see her back in the room, and she appeared to be doing well. I pointed to my cellphone, indicating she should check her messages. She smiled and waved. I mouthed "I love you" and walked to the nurse's station. Her nurse was seated at the nurses' station and smiled when she saw me approach her.

"She's responding well to the treatment. Her heart is marvelous!" she exclaimed. "We are still waiting on the test results from Wednesday evening, as it takes bacteria at least 24 to 48 hours to grow. Some take longer. She's been talking to all the nurses who go into her room. She really is amazing. We just love her."

I didn't say it, but I knew the feeling. Finding my usual stool by the small window, I texted Suzanne.

Lee: HEYYYY

Suz: I feel like we are talking in prison!

Lee: I told you the law would eventually catch up with you

Suz: Did you bring me a shiv?

I laughed out loud; she always made me laugh. It also suggested she was feeling better. Perhaps the antibiotic and lung exercises were helping her recover.

Lee: No, a cake with a file

Suz: How's your day been?

Lee: Seeing you smile made it all better

I wasn't being nice; it was the complete truth. I told her about talking to Matt, who said the Dream Team event was awesome, and he was proud of her and all she did at Kids Coast. They even said a prayer for Suzanne at the end of the service. Making it a bit lighter, I added that Bridget has never seen the movie *White Christmas*.

Suz: WHATTT?

Mentally, I committed to giving the movie on DVD to Bridget next December.

Suz: How's my hair look?

Be u ti ful?!!!

Lee: SEXY

I lied, but who wouldn't?

Suz: That's me

She laughed, then coughed violently. The last few days her coughing was continual and painful. And it seemed to be getting worse, but I didn't share my observation with her.

The doctor prescribed breathing exercises throughout the day to expand her lung capacity. One treatment was a simple ball in a vertical tube, which required the patient to blow into a tube to float the ball. The second was a noisy breathing machine that was run by a male respiratory technician in his sixties; it took about an hour from start to finish. Despite the pain, Suzanne continued the treatment every four hours. She did everything she could to get better; it was her way in life, always a calm, consistent fighter.

After one treatment, the technician pulled me aside and said, "Your wife … well, she's amazing. Her lung capacity is really low, which makes it hard to use my machine. I know it's painful. It literally stretches her lungs, and her lungs are inflamed now. Most of my patients quit after the first session, if they can even finish it. Not her; she just keeps going."

Special, she's so special, I thought to myself. That's my girl. I am so proud of her. She always inspired me with her actions.

And she always made me laugh. From her bed, Suzanne texted me a photo of the sink and toilet in her room that were partially covered by a privacy curtain.

Suz: Fancy sh@tter

She never cussed, not even on a one-to-one text with me. I texted back a short video of Eddie emptying the RV's portable potty into the street drain on *National Lampoon's Christmas Vacation.*

Suz: Love himmmmmm

I was laughing, and I could tell she was too, although obscured by her oxygen mask. She and I loved that movie and watched it every Christmas season. It was a toss-up whether she liked this movie more than *Planes, Trains, and Automobiles* or not. I changed the topic via text.

Lee: Oh, by the way...all the nurses have said "she is so nice"

As I anticipated, Suzanne's usual response was given.

Suz: Yeah right

Lee: The nurse showed me in your chart where one doctor stated "patient is very pleasant." She added she had never seen that type of comment before.

Suz: I wonder when we can do inperson

That touched my heart. It had been over twenty-four hours since we held hands, and she missed it, as did I. Suzanne would never have said, "I miss you"; she always took the indirect approach.

Lee: I think when they rule out TB. The infectious disease doctor should be here today

Earlier in the day, a CT scan revealed a large amount of fluid in her abdomen. They decided to draw it out to test it and to make her more comfortable.

Later that afternoon, the doctor would tell me, "It was a very large amount of fluid, about 400 milliliters."

I didn't understand the impact of his statement at the time, but would soon.

I held a card from Matt up to the small window for her to see. I opened it and took photos of the front, a Christmas tree, and inside these words, "Merry Christmas, Mom! Congratulations on your major award! Better than a leg lamp [a reference to one of our family's favorite movies, *The Christmas Story*]. Love you and praying for a quick recovery, Love, Matt."

It was near dinner time for the dogs at this point in the day, and I texted her.

Lee: I'll be back after dinner

Suz: U don't have to come back

Lee: I don't have to, but I will. I'll watch Pat and Vanna with you

The *Wheel of Fortune* had been our favorite TV show for thirty-five-plus years, and Pat Sajak and Vanna White were icons to us.

Lee: Do you want me to bring you anything?

Suz: Yes a black pair of leggings in 3rd row from left. If there's a thinner fabric. Just make sure there are no bleach spots or holes

In the sixties, mothers taught their kids to never leave the house wearing underwear with holes, because if you get in a car accident, the ambulance driver will think the family is trashy. Mothers were more concerned about clean underwear than the medical capabilities of the ambulance drivers. I waved to her as I walked away.

Lee: I LOVE YOU. I'll see you after dinner

Suz: TY. ❤ you more

She told me that often, and I always liked hearing those words from her. I drove home and walked the exuberant dogs around the block. When I returned home with them, they wanted food in their dinner bowls. Even dogs have priorities depending on the hour of the day.

My phone chimed with a new text; it was one of the Kids Coast staff members. She asked me to tell Suzanne everyone was praying for her quick recovery and hoped to see her next week at church. Apparently, the Kids Coast staff members were shocked when they learned Suzanne was in the ICU, and they were not sure how to handle the situation.

Suz: Dr just left. May be here for a couple days. May be moved to WA. Going to give me heavy antibiotics. You can still come back up when finished there

It was her way of saying she really needed me to be with her. She didn't like hearing it would be a couple more days in the hospital.

Suz: They put me on oxygen

This struck me as odd because she had been on oxygen since the first night. I assumed she meant more oxygen, but I didn't ask.

Suz: Skip the shake, I'm not hungry

Now I knew she was uneasy, as she didn't eat the shake they had for her. As the dogs ate, I searched for her clothes. Easy to find them. She was always neat and arranged her clothes hanging in the closet by color. She'd requested that when I found the leggings, I would text her.

Lee: henry pooped a big 'n

Anyone with a dog understands the importance of this statement.

Suz: that's my boy

She replied with a smiling face.

Lee: leaving in a few

Suz: Pls don't feel like you need to come up. Don't need anything TY.! still uncomfortable in right lung.

Even after all those years together, I think she was still surprised I really loved her so much. I believe it was her traumatic past. I knew exactly how she felt, and I made sure I was always there for her. It was her love language to hear it from me.

Lee: ok I'll be up a few. Want to make sure there's no single men in there

I texted, hoping to lighten the mood.

Suz: Ummmmm you're safe

Suzanne never wanted me to worry about her. I would later realize how thankful I was for the ability to send a text to her phone. It allowed us to communicate constantly because we always talked. And I would soon appreciate having our discussions documented in that way, so I can always go back and reread them.

I walked into the ICU and saw the nurses had left the stool in place by the prison window to Suzanne's isolation room. She was awake and saw me sit down at the window.

Lee: HEYYYY

Suz: Hey. How was your afternoon!

Lee: Look what I got! It's a fan plugged into the laptop by my chair

Suz: You on the hot seat?

Lee: No, one of the nurses is in menopause and needs it. How you feeling?

My stool was also in front of the nurse's station. I quickly learned there are no secrets, and nothing is sacred when the nurses are talking to each other. Even at my advanced age, I learned a few new things about women during this time.

Suz: Better. right lung not as sore. I went to potty and brushed my teeth. The nurse propped me up and I told her 'hey I feel better' don't know what did it but I'll take it' she said.

Lee: good!

Suz: 127/96 BP just now

I could tell she was proud of herself for what she could do. Suzanne was uncomfortable around doctors, ever since having an infant heart murmur as a young child. Seeing doctors brought back unpleasant memories for her. When she saw a doctor or nurse, her blood pressure would shoot to 166/96. She always had low blood pressure, typically 118/70.

Lee: she said your right side should be better tomorrow after your lungs have expanded. go girl!

Suz: for some reason I thought it would expand quickly

I knew she was disappointed at these results.

Lee: new nurse very nice. Said you're very nice to work with. She said she knows you're uncomfortable so please let her know if you want to get up. Sit in chair, walk a little–all will help you (may hurt at first) also let her know if you need a pillow, a drink, etc. she's very pleasant

Suz: ok she's a very nice lady Allison
She was here at 330 last night

Lee: nurses and doctors say lungs heal slowly

Suz: Ugh

When she said "Ugh," it meant she was really feeling defeated. In the rare instances she felt bad, Suzanne would rarely speak. No complaining, only "UGH."

Lee: dang long day

Suz: she works 7 pm to 7 am. she was in room when I came up last night

Lee: rough. let me know if you are tired and I'll leave

Suz: Nope I'm good. Feel better

with lung better. Miserable before

We traded news about Betsy seeking a new car; her current car had high mileage and needed engine oil weekly. Matt stopped by our house to make dinner and catch up on life. He was happy living in Hanahan and liked the house he bought a couple of months ago. Matt was planning to be a trail boss on the Seacoast Church Men's Hike in the spring. All this news made Suzanne happy.

Told her Betsy surprised me with a birthday cake as I was walking the dogs outside. She came in and all of us had cake and ice cream, thanks to Suzanne's stocking the freezer regularly. It was a nice surprise, and I wanted to get back to see Suzanne once we were done. Fortunately, the nurses ignored the nine-p.m. cut-off for visitors and let me stay all day and night. That's another good reason to partner with the nurses. They even offered to microwave some of their dinners for me. The nurses were amazing.

I waved to Suzanne as I sat on my stool. The fan was gone, and I assumed the nurse in menopause was on another shift. Suzanne waved and pointed at her phone. She texted me a photo of a Styrofoam cup filled with Diet Coke and nugget ice, like Sonic's, that she loved.

It was those small things I loved about her so much. Suzanne would get excited over a fountain drink if it had nugget ice. Wisely, I had purchased a nugget ice machine for the house, and you would have thought I gave her a five-carat diamond ring. Suzanne continued to text me.

Suz: From Allison! Fun ish ice

Lee: Yea! want some juice?

Suz: Got a water bottle, cranberry juice and 2 vanilla pudding

Lee: PUDDING! Geez

It was one of the few things we always disagreed about. Suzanne loved any kind of pudding, and I never liked any kind of pudding. I couldn't even fake it and pretend to enjoy it when she ordered it at a restaurant.

Suz: Look

She proudly displayed the plastic cups of pudding.

Lee: twin pack!

Suz: ate some soup. did the trick

Lee: good!!! you must be starved

Suz: I was. Good now

Lee: they have applesauce too!

Suz: yours is better. You need to go home and get some sleep. Huge day for you today

Lee: tired? I love sitting here

I wanted Suzanne to know there was no place I would rather be than by her side. Even if it meant outside the window of her prison cell, I would never leave her side.

Suz: and tomorrow is your big medicare 65 woop woop

Lee: I'm not 65 till 11:50pm!!!

Suz: Rules

Lee: I cant bear it (medicare)

Suz: It happens to the best of us

Getting older never bothered me; I'll take as many birthdays as possible. But I was not excited about Medicare and its related government inefficiency.

Suzanne and I never really cared about getting older. The only birthday she dreaded was turning thirty years old, figuring life was all downhill from there. It didn't help that my neighbor nailed an 8 x10 foot sheet of plywood with the words "SUZANNE CARRICK IS 30" in large letters to the roof of our house on the Air Force base. Several floodlights were also nailed to the roof to illuminate this fact all night. She disliked sixty-five, only because she was forced to enroll in Medicare. She was eleven months older than me and weathered all the life events first. She was not happy to have no choice but to be on a government-run program. Too much paperwork, limited options, too difficult to work with, and we quickly learned that the only thing they really care about was limiting services to save money.

Lee: do you want to get up or move?

Suz: Not just yet. I'll have to pee in a lil bit. I don't want to bother them too much

Lee: they are fine

Suz: they're busy

This was not accurate, as there were only five patients and three nurses on duty. Typically, they assigned one nurse to two patients. Her nurse didn't have any other patients that shift, but that was Suzanne, never wanting to cause a fuss. I knew she had one nurse assigned to her, and it was on the oversized whiteboard on the wall by the nurse's station. I noticed all the nurses would check on Suzanne throughout their shift.

Lee: they all like you

Suz: They're very kind and compassionate people

Lee: I think they like talking to "nice people" [like you] as it's refreshing

Suz: Prob[ably] Really you should head home now. It's 10. You for dogs tonight and tomorrow morning

Lee: well you're a year older than me so I guess I have to listen

Suz: Yup. You need some rest more than anything

I remember thinking how much I love this girl.

Lee: Allison said it sometimes takes 24 hours to [blood test] results from downtown. So 'no results' means 'not completed yet

Suz: Did she say anything about the blood work today! They were looking for something specific

Lee: I'll ask

Suz: can you ask her if she can lay me flat?

Suzanne refused to push the call button to summon the nurses, thinking it was rude.

Lee: you have a ZERO G bed!

I was referring to the adjustable bed we had bought a few years prior. The only "medical" condition she ever had was that her back would hurt at night when sleeping. The adjustable bed worked perfectly for her. The Zero G position raised her back and knees at the same time, and it was her favorite. The bed also could vibrate, providing some level of massage, which she called the "jiggle" that would help her sleep.

Suz: Miss my jiggle

Lee: okay I'm going home. I'll see you in the am

Suz: ❤❤❤❤❤❤ thanks for everything

Lee: sure! love you too

As I walked out, I remembered the doctor saying the fluid around her lungs pushes against the heart, and the heart reacts by adding more fluid. He said it wasn't an issue because her heart was strong, but the drain would remain to keep fluid off as the lungs healed, so she would be more comfortable. They had a drain tube running from her to a collection bag underneath her bed; I could see it from my prison window and would keep watching it. Less fluid would mean her lungs were healing.

As I drove home, I was getting a bit more excited about Suzanne coming home soon. The doctors told me several times during the day the types of viruses and bacteria they eliminated as the cause of her pneumonia. I parked in the garage and walked up the stairs into the dark house. I fed the dogs, and they fell asleep quickly.

Suzanne and I talked often during the evenings when we were home. Often it was trivial, but we liked conversing; it connected us physically. I always liked the sound of her voice, always kind and comforting. I also enjoyed knowing she would spend all her evenings with me. Tonight, it was quiet again. Too quiet for me.

SIX

Ups and Downs
Friday, December 9th

I awoke early that morning. My hand searched for my cellphone, knocking it onto the carpet under my bed while trying to grab for it. The bright blue screen revealed its location. A long, uncharacteristic text filled the screen.

Suz: morning

Suz: Remember how good I felt when I was sitting up and texting with you? That went downhill fast when I tried to lay down. Couldn't get comfortable. Allison was watching my vitals and saw they were high. She came in about 2 and asked if I had gotten any rest. Said not really I was so uncomfortable. She asked dr if I could have something some pain since it was 8-10 [on the pain scale]. She called in a big gun that worked right away.

Pain in the 8-10 range shocked me, then my heart broke. First mention of any pain, and I realized again how useless I was in this situation. All I could do was pray and get dressed as quickly as possible. We continued texting as I walked the dogs.

Suz: Slept good till she came in for blood at 6. Said I may have lung scope procedure today, saw it in notes but not sure

Suz: Havent seen anyone today yet. Could you pls bring fresh clothes today?

Lee: wow. How is pain now?

Suz: Much better

Lee: I checked your test results. The 'basic metabolic panel' you only have one [Ige] that is a little high. Two that were high are normal now.

Lee: henry pooped last night

Suz: Not this AM! He will after breakfast

Suz: Btw HB! [Happy Birthday]

Lee: I got 14 more hours!

Suz: Hahah stretch it!

I loved to make her laugh and would do and say almost anything to hear her bold laughter.

Lee: henry is missing you, keeps looking for you

Suz: I miss him too. Cant wait to get home

Lee: I'm tired so I'm not coming over

Suz: ok get some rest

Lee: KIDDING Need fresh drawers fresh pants?

Suz: yes. Respiratory lady told me this AM I have to cough 3 negative lung samples then you can come in. Today is day 2. working hard to bring up junk so U can come in!

Lee: GO GIRL!

When I returned home with the dogs, I logged onto the hospital systems to view her latest test results. As I reviewed and compared the data, I was grateful for the technology and access to the information. I continued texting her updates on her test results.

Lee: soooo. All your numbers are improving. Here is list of molecular (flu, RSV etc) that you do NOT have! NEGATIVE! all the influenzas, RSV, covid, Bordetella (hahah) are negative

Bordetella was funny because dogs get the same vaccines to be boarded in a kennel.

Suz: Good

Lee: Yes BORDATELLA test 🐶 I checked your chart. No word on the tests they did in all the little booze bottles

Lee: I think it has to sit and "grow" for several hours

Suz: Ohhhhhh

Lee: what did doc say?

Suz: Dr just said they don't want to have to do the scope. So keep spitting

The "scope" was a bronchoscopy to view the airways and diagnose lung disease. It's a long, flexible tube inserted through the throat into the lungs for a biopsy. The doctor didn't want to use it, as it could spread the infection further in her lungs.

As soon as I arrived at the ICU, I found her doctor. He didn't smile as he explained her current condition. It wasn't clear to me why he seemed so concerned. I assumed he had a long day and much was on his mind. I ignored my assessment wanting to believe she was improving.

Lee: he [doctor] said you are improving. And lungs are slow to heal

Suz: that nurse I was talking to was the dietitian. She said "you look good except your BMI is LOW"

That was welcome news to Suzanne, as she always worried about her weight, like most ladies I suppose. Even though she was always within ten pounds of her high school weight, she consistently considered herself "massive." Knowing she would like that news, I replied back to her.

Lee: heyyyyy

Suz: heyyyyy

She responded with a silent laugh as she looked at me; it was awful to see her and not hear her voice. I missed the intimacy of talking to her face to face.

Lee: so she [dietitian] is adding chocolate Ensure to your daily schedule to give you protein. I knew you would LOVE that

Suz: Oh no, memories of your ma

My mother's life of poor diet and no exercise caused a myriad of health issues late in her life. She loved that nasty, thick liquid. Suz and I tried it once, and we gagged.

Suz: My nurse said I get a shot in the belly today to prevent blood clots. Said I might not like it. Med[icine] burns going in

Lee: Both doctors said you are improving. They have ruled out all viruses. Narrowing down bacteria. Thinkin it may be fungal

Suz: ate the scrambled eggs and one bite of French toast

French toast was her lifelong breakfast favorite, which she prepared this delicacy with equal amounts of toast and syrup.

Suz: Got my belly shot. Wasn't too bad. Burned a lil bit

I was glad she couldn't see my face through the small window because it became harder to fight back tears at her pain. It was heartbreaking, but I would never tell her that. Suzanne was so strong, so positive, so faithful. She never doubted Jesus and always increased my faith with her example of faith.

Suz: Nurse said don't hesitate to call if I need anything. Keeps her out of the other patient's room. [the other patient is] A handful

I noticed nurses were gathered around either their station or Suzanne's room during my time there.

Suz: think about something we can do for this [ICU] floor staff after we leave

Lee: of course. They are awesome

Lee: Dr Parker said "she's a dream. Such a pleasure. We'll take good care of her. " Said he hopes to clear the tuberculosis in 24 hours and get you into a regular room. Says you still need oxygen

Suz: Yea I still get winded getting up. Dr Parker said I will be on antibiotic for a year

I knew Suzanne didn't like to hear that news. She never took prescription medications and despised pills and vaccines. I chose to use the doctor's exact words when texting her.

Lee: lung doc said you should feel better in a week. And much much better in less than a month

Suz: oh good wish it was sooner but I'll take that. And end in sight

Lee: I think you'll recover quicker. You don't like being sick. You'll overcome it

Suz: YES

Lee: and you're very healthy to start. They all said it's a big plus for you

Suz: Thank u Jesus. Hey do you want to give Stephen [her brother] a call later today? Just to let him know. He texted me a picture from his walk yesterday but I didn't respond

Lee: yes I'll call. 13 more hours [till my 65th birthday]

Suz: Hahaha

I texted her some of the prayers the ladies were sending to me.

Suz: those gals are unbelievable

Lee: I'm going home to let dogs out. Be back in a few

Suz: Tell boys [her dogs] ❤❤❤. Thanks for everything. Hey can you bring back some acetone polish remover, cotton pads and the 30$ nail file? I'm going to work on removing finger polish and gel so they can use it for oxygen meter.

The pulse oximeter was connected to her finger, and the oxygen saturation reading was dropping, down to 92%. The nurses didn't believe that was correct, so they asked her to remove her acrylic, aka fake, fingernails.

Lee: yes. Talked to the VW salesman and he found a car for Betsy

Suz: Okayyyy. Also can you bring a pink bottle with green lid Clinique face toner in my bathroom cabinet? And a few cotton pads for that. And...a 5 inch of Reynolds wrap, not the cut sheets of foil TY TY

I stepped away from the window and waved as I left the ICU. When I got home, I texted a photo of my birthday cake to Suzanne.

Lee: breakfast

Suz: You deserve it

She responded, and I pictured her laughing at me.

Lee: Im kidding

Suz: Im not.

Suzanne had a sweet tooth as long as I knew her. Although her favorite breakfast when she was younger was cold leftover pizza.

Finishing scrambled eggs, not cake, I texted her a photo of the dishwasher about ten percent full. One of her funny quirks was overfilling the dishwasher to not waste electricity and water. We both had holdovers from our parents growing up in the 1930s.

Lee: running dishwasher. And it's NOT FULL

Suz: I'll forgive you this time

Lee: I'm running it tomorrow too

I envisioned her shaking her head and showing me an expression of despair. Her Depression-era mother would not approve of such wasteful activity.

Suz: take your time coming back I might try to snooze a lil.

She texted me at 4:06 p.m., after she took a nap. I walked the dogs. Returning home, I checked her medical chart online. Still all normal, except the Ipe remained high.

How can her red and blood cell count be normal? Everything is normal.

Based on her consistently positive results, I told myself she was getting better; it was the only logical explanation.

Suz: Do you want to chill at home and come over after you feed the boys [at 6:00]?

Lee: ok. I moustache you a question. How ya doing

Suz: They say I am requiring more oxygen so bigger tubing. I'll show you my new toy. It's a breathing device I have to suck on ten times an hour. It will make my lungs stronger

I logged off and drove the five miles to the hospital. The cold, overcast day made everything in sight a shade of gray. Leaving my car in the empty parking lot, I passed through the empty emergency room entrance and across empty hallways to the elevator for the ICU. Light yellow walls brightened the hallways despite the gloomy weather.

Once at Suzanne's room, I slid onto my stool and gazed immediately at the monitor: 92%. Next, I looked at the light green digital readout above the oxygen port, which now read 10%; yesterday it was 2%. Realizing that more oxygen flowing through her mask was not improving her 92% oxygen saturation rate, I was increasingly uneasy about her condition. She could not see my expression, which would have conveyed my concern.

Lee: How you feeling

She texted me a photo of black bean soup in a Styrofoam cup.

Suz: Little tired but might be because I'm doing this breathing machine and spitting up stuff. Might feel better after the black beans

Lee: Oh yes. It's good stuff

She texted me a photo of chocolate milk in nugget ice.

Suz: Ensure yummmm. Yea its really not that bad

My peripheral vision caught a person walking toward me in the quiet hallway of the ICU. Dr. Parker slowed as he passed her room. He looked at her then walked to me, offering an update. Perhaps he knew I noticed the increased oxygen flow from 2% to 10%.

Suz: Did you get any info from Dr Parker?

Lee: Dr Parker said you needed more oxygen. He wanted a chest x-ray to see if anything has changed. And he wanted to compare the ct scan from American Imaging [taken 3 weeks ago] to compare. Also wants the fake nail off of course. Says it could be the issue.

Suz: ok women want to look good for Dr. S

I laughed. Dr. Parker was a nice man with good manners, and, yes, he was a handsome dude. She was such a lady, always wanted to appear nice in public. Not over the top like so many women today, only a touch of lipstick, rouge, and top eyeliner. She was a simple girl, which I loved so much about Suzanne.

Her nurse handed a card with "Momma" written on the red envelope to Suzanne. She tore off the end, pulling the card out of the envelope. She held the card with Snoopy on the front, reading the inside slowly. She glanced at me and waved the card, as if to fan her face.

Suz: tell Betsy I love her

Lee: she misses you

The nurses' holistic approach included the entire environment for their patient, including me. My presence helped Suzanne's attitude. Few people visited the ICU; usually, I was the only visitor. The few who visited spent less than five minutes on the floor. My respect for nurses continued to increase with this perspective.

Suz: whatcha ya talkin to nurses about?

Lee: They asked if I could help out in the ICU since I'm here all day. I said I know how to sweep floors and they said "we'll take it!"

I saw her laugh and shake her head, likely thinking, *Oh my, that man is such a mess.*

Suz: Would you tell them I took the oxygen meter off to file my fingernail?

Lee: All the nurses told me they feel bad you're stuck in that [isolation] room, and they added "She is still so nice."

That type of comment was typical when people were around Suzanne. It made me so proud of her, so grateful she was my girl. I knew how lucky I was every day, and I thanked Jesus for her daily at a minimum.

Suz: Yes they are awesome and usually very timely

Lee: new test results from this afternoon from Parker. IGC tests level of infection in the body as the antibodies present to fight the infection. Normal range is 700 – 1600, yours is 789. Go girl!

Suz: Do you want to ask one of the ladies to look and see if this works pls?

I always marveled at her kind spirit. Always asked, always polite, always loving. Such an amazing woman. Suzanne was acting as if she were at home on a sunny day.

Lee: oh Parker said they think they have isolated the infection. They have some more tests to do. Says its slow growing and hard to find in the lab

Suz: ohhhh good

Lee: Its not TB related and not contagious. Is soil based. It's natural

Suz: Of course! Go big or go home. I've always been different!

Different, always. Never fit into the fast-paced Virginia-DC metropolitan; simple and together was her joy.

Automatic heavy double doors swooshed open, granting access to Matt. As he passed Room #1, he waved at his mom through the window. The shock on his game face was evident as he saw where she was. Her face lit up, and she held out her arms, wishing to hug him. Texting and hand motions ensued as I walked away to give them time, thinking constantly about how good it would be to have her back at home.

Later that day, during Suzanne's testing regime, I mentioned to her nurses at their station that it was hard to be apart from her for the last three days.

Nodding in agreement, an experienced nurse, Debbie, remarked, "Just be glad it's not COVID still. That was awful for families. No one was even allowed in the ICU or the hospital. People were so alone. People died without ever seeing their families and friends. We had to be their families. Often, we were the only ones in the room when the patient passed away."

"It was so stressful," a young nurse added. "It was terrible for us. We had strict rules about what we could and could not do. We had to limit visiting patients. It broke our hearts. People lay in their beds alone. Many nurses burned out and quit during that terrible time. We had been dealing with all types of diseases, and now all the rules were changed. Made me mad. I experienced guilt for months because I couldn't take care of my patients."

Reliving those years was difficult for the nurses. After a pause, they focused on Suzanne. "She really is amazing. We know how uncomfortable she is, yet she never complains. Most patients in pain take it out on us."

It was almost midnight and quiet on the floor. I asked to speak with the charge nurse, adding. “I only want to tell her how awesome you guys are.” The nurse at the desk smiled in relief.

A few minutes later, a nurse with a slight smile approached from a side room. Glancing at the nurse’s name tag, I told Rebecca, about the professionalism and kindness of her nurses. She questioned Suzanne’s positive attitude and remarked that Suzanne was kind to all the nurses, which rarely happens. Noticing my curious expression, Rebecca explained that most patients were in the ICU due to a tragic event, such as a car accident or heart attack. Fear and anger were common, which resulted in patients and family venting their emotions on the undeserving nurses. Now, my respect for these women and men soared even higher.

Rebecca commented, “Suzanne is unique, quite unique. She’s been pleasant from the minute she arrived. The nurses don’t understand how she could be so kind despite her condition.”

The term “her condition” did not register in my mind enough to warrant me asking her more questions. I explained to Rebecca that Suzanne was a Jesus follower for many years, as was I.

A large smile appeared on her face. We learned we both attended the same church and realized we were in sync. Pausing, then looking straight into my eyes, Rebecca said my wife was making a huge impact on the nursing staff. The nurses who were Christians said their faith was restored by Suzanne’s faith and positive attitude.

A simple act of kindness was making a big impact, I thought.

Rebecca added that the nurses who were not believers were asking, "What does she know that we don't know?" I was stunned. Jesus was at work on the ICU floor.

Suzanne was in a location where nurses were treated terribly by ill patients and families who were scared and frustrated. They dealt with patients' anger in parallel with severe medical trauma. Nurses have seen the worst and saved lives.

However, the last three days were different for the nurses. In a quiet ICU, this polite, faithful sixty-five-year-old lady broke through their tough, protective outer shells and touched their hearts. My eyes watered, overwhelmed with emotion. This was different; I never witnessed this situation in the last forty-eight years I knew Suzanne. This was a different experience.

SEVEN

Divide & Conquer
Saturday, December 10th

Hoping I slept all night, my eyes wanted to remain closed in the morning darkness. Mental exhaustion was worse than physical, but my hand instinctively picked up my cellphone from the nightstand. I quickly shaved and skipped breakfast, knowing I could grab a cup of coffee at the nurses' station. I exited the elevator, and the ICU doors opened before I could press the button. The nurses saw me coming and didn't hesitate to open the doors. I waved to Suzanne, held up my cellular phone, and started texting.

Lee: heyyy

Suz: Rough night. Lots of coughing

Such a statement was atypical for Suzanne, as she was telling me her pain was worse. I struggled to see her expression as she lay in the bed motionless.

Suz: It all started again when I did
the spit cut [for a bronchial test] for
the 3rd time at 5 PM

Dr. Parker paused by the room to chat with me as I sat on my stool in the ICU hallway. He visited her several times a day at this point.

Lee: Doctor said they are narrowing it down. They have a specialist looking at your case to help figure out what it is

Suz: They had me do the lung blowing machine 10 times every hour and it made me cough too

The breathing machine was as big as a kitchen oven, but portable, and loud as ten vacuum cleaners running simultaneously. The forced air being pumped into her weak lungs brought severe pain across Suzanne's body. But she never quit and volunteered for extra treatments to help speed her lung recovery along. As the technician left her room, he said Suzanne was the first person to ask for extra treatments because the machine was painful, even though effective.

Lee: Doctor read the CT scan from American Imaging. And he says it helps them understand what is going on. It's a slow growing bacterium. He says they hope to know what it is today

Suz: Nurse gave me a TB test under skin because they didn't get results on the 3rd spit cup. May take 24 hours to know.

My hopes for progress were not valid, as all Suzanne's effort yesterday afternoon was for naught.

Lee: I thought they knew it wasn't TB, but all of this connected somehow. So probably no sleep last night?

Suz: Not much. Had to sleep sitting up and that doesn't work well. Then started coughing around 3 am and she brought me cough meds as scheduled at 4 am and then did blood work, which lasted till 5 bc she couldn't find a vein and had to get another nurse to find it, which she did

I grimaced, knowing Suzanne hated needles and doctors in general. Health issues as a young girl required frequent hospital visits, which gave her "White Coat Syndrome."

Suz: on top of coughing, my nose got congested and made it harder to breath

I released a deep sigh; glad she could not hear me. She needed a break to feel better.

Suz: Ended up moving to the chair at 3 because I couldn't get comfortable in bed

As I was sitting on my stool texting Suzanne, one of the doctors stopped to provide his thoughts to me on a tuberculosis diagnosis. He asked similar questions and received the same responses from me. I thought it odd they were still asking about tuberculosis.

Suz: anything going on out in the hallway?

Lee: the specialist was there. He asked the same questions, said he thinks its TB (which is easily treatable) or a cousin of TB (the soil based one). He said TB is uncommon but it does occur. They are going to give you a steroid to help fight the inflammation. to clear the TB and the cousin are easily treatable

I was confused now though, as they said since she checked in, Suzanne didn't have TB, but now the specialist said it was. No wonder they avoided going into her room.

Suz: gotcha

Suz: it was crazy busy here last night. At 915 I asked night nurse if she should come back around 10 and help me clean up change clothes for bed. The little tech girl came back at 1040. I asked her if it was busy. She said OMG yea. Friday's are always busy but Saturday nights are much slower

I shook my head in disbelief. Then, chatter at the nurses' station confirmed a car wreck and drinking had brought patients in.

Lee: interesting. Friday must be "party night"

Suz: Yes or payday

Lee: $$$$ = trouble

She waved a thumbs-up at me.

Lee: did you change clothes?

Suz: yea check it out

She threw the sheets back to show me and was so proud of herself.

Suz: clean clothes and clean sheets

I could see her smile behind her oxygen mask.

Lee: new unders too?

She peeled the sheets back higher and grinned.

Lee: YESSSS

She always said I was a fourteen-year-old boy.

Lee: whats for breakfast?

Suz: cheese omelet and breakfast potatoes and ICED tea!

Her favorite morning beverage was iced tea, and the nurses brewed some for her in their kitchen instead of using the hospital cafeteria.

Suz: they weighed me at 4 am last night and I am the same as when I

was admitted on Wednesday.
That's good I haven't lost weight while here

Lee: good! Slim and sexy

Suz: Matt's card is amazing. Very thoughtful and lovingly said

She paused and reflected on Matt, who moved to Charleston a year ago.

Suz: He looks happy now

Suz: that's all I want for the kids. Happy and healthy

Lee: I agree

I nodded my head as I typed my message to her. My thoughts drifted back to her.

Lee: I sure miss talking to you and holding your hand

Suz: Me too. Hopefully soon you can come inside my humble abode

Lee: I noticed that the nurses are coming into your room without the protective gear

Suz: Thanks for bringing all the goods this AM. Bonus – choc milk

Suzanne loved chocolate milk but reserved it for special occasions only. In her anteroom, a nurse donned protective gear, then carried a dinner tray into her room. Suzanne and the nurse were talking, but I could not hear them. It was a silent movie, a movie that continued to stream all day, every day.

Lee: Why don't you eat now?

I mimicked using a fork to eat in front of the small window separating us.

Suz: Waiting for the respirator to come in first

Suz: How's everything at the house? Any good mail? Did any of the journey toys come yet?

Our church provided backpacks for foster children to meet basic needs when they "journeyed" to a new home. They asked the congregation to purchase a backpack and fill it with the listed items for boys and girls, from babies to seventeen years old. Suzanne made a dozen journey bags; all year, she purchased items for the bags.

Lee: yes on journey bags but I haven't opened all the boxes yet. The baseball bat is due on Monday

Suz: Don't forget to pay the credit card bill

Suzanne took over paying our monthly bills several years ago, never wanting to be a military widow unable to manage a household if I were to pass.

Lee: Yes I paid the bill

As we texted, Dr. Parker walked through the vestibule into her room, his face mask below his chin, demonstrating kindness to allow her to see his expressions. I watched another silent movie as they talked, both of them smiling. After a few minutes, he waved and left her room, stopping by my stool by the small window. Said he gave Suzanne all the facts, adding a steroid to calm the lungs so the antibiotic could work better. He started to walk to his next appointment when he paused, turned, and looked directly into my eyes and said, "She's amazing."

Lee: He said the steroids he ordered are like firefighters. They will quiet down the mess in there

I could see her laugh, wishing I could hear her as well.

Lee: He is a believer. He said all people have three things; Spiritual health, Physical health and Mental health or positive attitude. He said you have GREAT spiritual health and GREAT positive mental health which will make a tremendous difference to help you get your strong physical health back. He said the two you have are HUGE helpers. Makes all the difference

Suz: Makes sense

Lee: he said you're awesome, just awesome

Suz: he's pretty great too

I could tell she was smiling as she typed.

Lee: I am praising God for him and all the others [doctors and nurses]

Suz: Yes

She was a bit misty as we tested, as I peered through the window at her. I was tearing up, too. Where do they find these doctors and nurses? Why do they work so hard? I didn't know the answer, but I knew Jesus did.

Suz: on new oxygen machine now. Blows a ton of air

Lee: You may start floating like a balloon!

Suz: Got steroid injection

Suz: I just did my lung toy. At first, I was going up to 500 and then at the end of 10 times I had it up 750

Using the lung exerciser was difficult and made Suzanne's lungs hurt, but nothing would deter her from doing everything possible to get home soon. Suzanne texted me a photo of the lung toy, and after seeing it, I tried to make the situation light and texted her response.

Lee: looks like a drink at the [Disney] polyneisan [Hotel]

Suz: Haha Poly drink

Suz: I remember my mom having one of these [lung exerciser] and also giving herself the treatment that looks like she's vaping

Her mother smoked heavily all her life, which resulted in significant lung issues as she aged. I remember seeing the many breathing devices on her mother's table. Made me feel ill to think Suzanne did everything right and was now having to use the same devices.

I was not surprised at how hard she worked because that was her style. My respect climbed; this woman truly was amazing.

Lee: go girl

Lee: I knew you were strong, but now you AMAZE me

Suz: Working on it hard

Lee: Doctor said that will make the difference. So many patients are difficult and don't do what the doctors ask.

Not Suzanne, she was a hundred percent committed.

Suz: [nurse] did another blood draw but can't remember what for

It seemed like they were constantly conducting blood tests with Suzanne; they did a full blood panel every four hours. I remembered checking her test results online again this morning, which continued to be normal. I dismissed it as typical, since they were looking for the bacteria.

When I spoke to her brother Steve, he told me how much he loved her and all the things he liked about her.

Lee: I talked to Steve and he is praying for you. He thinks a lot of you

Suz: he better, I'm his best sister

That made me laugh because she was his only sister. Still had a sense of humor despite the pain and discomfort. *That's my girl.*

Looking at my watch, I realized several hours had passed, so I drove to our house to walk the dogs. While I was at home, Suzanne texted me that she had two gift cards for Vineyard Vines that would expire in a few days.

Suz: You need to use the gift cards to buy some things for yourself. I don't need anything. I think I left them [gift cards] on the [kitchen] island

Finding the two gift cards, I texted a photo for confirmation to her. She never wanted to lose money or miss a good sale.

Suz: They are having an outlet sale. Pls go in and find something you like. They have some long sleeve shirts. I don't want to use them. And it doesn't have to be LS shirts. Get anything else you like And look for the code

Knowing I would return to the hospital, she texted a request.

Suz: Favor – would you go by Chic-fil and get me a peppermint shake pls? No whip pls?

She loved whipped cream, but that added about ten calories to the 600 calories already in the thick, creamy milkshake.

I texted a "thumbs-up," followed by a text reminder about the Army-Navy football game that day. During the war, she volunteered at USO, providing direct support to the Army and Air Force men and women deployed in Afghanistan. We often visited the Naval Academy to watch the Midshipmen play football. Their stadium provided a somber reminder of the many sacrifices made by the brave men and women since the founding of our nation. And yet it was so alive and joyful as the teams competed on the field. I reminded Suzanne so she could ask the nurse to put the game on the TV in her hospital room.

Lee: Army-Navy Game. 2:00 pregame, 3:00 kickoff

Suz: oh TY I forgot

I drove up to the Chick-fil-A restaurant and placed her order. I texted her a photo of the Chick-fil-A drive-through window and then her peppermint milkshake sitting in the cup holder.

Suz: Yum!

Suz: 3-0 Navy

Lee: Your breathing technician was in the air force in Vietnam

We had a special respect for those men and women who served in 'Nam. During high school, the Vietnam War was on the news constantly. The devastation was heartbreaking; it was the main reason I joined the Air Force. I saw what they were going through while I was in high school. The only way I knew I could help was to wear a uniform and do my part.

As I walked into the ICU hallway, I saw the game on the TV in her room. She saw me and waved.

Suz: 7-3 navy

Suz: 7-3 army

Suz: hell i don't know

I chuckled because she never cussed. And I was running late and missing the beginning of the game, which was action-filled.

Lee: The respiratory tech said your lungs are starting to open up [due to the machine exercises]

Suz: Yes thank you Lord

Her doctor had checked on her when she was doing the breathing exercises on the machine. He stopped by my stool to give me an update and check on her. Typically, he would stand outside her glass doors and gaze at her. I always wondered what he was thinking. I texted Suzanne his comment to me.

Lee: "She'll work her way out of here. No one likes that machine and most refuse to use it. It's the best thing to help"

Suz: machine is really loud. And when you plug it into your nose it's

like a fire hose of air going into
your nose

Suz: I think I'm pretty much
confined to bed with this machine

Suz: nurse is bringing lighter gown,
turned the AC down

She paused as she watched the game. The thoughtful nurses opened her curtains so I could watch the game with her. It was another silent movie, but I didn't care as long as I was with her.

Dr. Parker stopped by again to chat while we watched the game, checking on her more frequently than expected. He was there at least twelve hours daily; something about her intrigued him. On this visit, I asked him where he went to school.

Suz: Who is my doctor rooting for
[in the game]

Lee: Doesn't care

Lee: your doctor grew up in
Roanoake [Virginia]. Went to VT
[Virginia Tech] Med school. Very
nice man. Met his wife in college.
Got married. She wanted to move
back to Erie [PA] to be near family.
A year later she said get me out.
We gotta go south. Been here a bit
over a year.

Suzanne nodded as she switched between watching the game and reading her cellphone texts from me. Her nurse stopped to tell me she was split between Army and Navy, as she was Navy, and her fiancé was Army.

Lee: nurse is split

Suz: Yea she told me

Suz: shake was good TY

I looked at her, and she gave me a thumbs-up smiling.

Lee: You didn't save me any?

That was a lifelong inside joke between us. Suzanne was always generous except for desserts, which always made me laugh because it was uncharacteristic of her. That sweet tooth of hers was king. After we finished dinner at a restaurant, Suzanne would order dessert for two reasons: #1) You can always take it home, and #2) never turn away banana or bread pudding.

When she told the server her choice of dessert, the server always asked, "Would you like two plates?"

To which Suzanne would immediately respond, "Oh no! I don't share well!" and then would give me the "Don't mess with me" expression.

I loved that silly girl so much; she always made me laugh. The servers always got a laugh out of it, too.

I looked at Suzanne as she watched television in her hospital room. My mind drifted away from the game and back to her situation. This woman, whom I had known and loved my entire life, continued to amaze me. She was the kindest, most loving person I had ever known. I could not wait to see her face to face and drive her home.

Lee: I'm so proud of you working so hard

Suz: I am getting out of here as soon as I can

Suz: you can't stay late tonight

I nodded, though I knew I wasn't leaving anytime soon. I learned how to walk the ICU hallway where she could not see me. I was quiet and never bothered the nurses, so they let me stay as long as I wanted. My routine was to slowly walk from one end of the hall to the other. Praying mostly. For Suzanne. For the nurses. For the doctors.

It was easy to hide as the nurses dimmed the hall lights around eight p.m. I just couldn't go home; if we didn't have the dogs at our house, I would never have left.

Suzanne and I were always together, and that was the best part of our marriage. Often, we would sit together, each reading separately with no conversation. We didn't have to talk, but we had to be in the same room. She needed to be within my view. Often, when I would pause reading and check on her, she was looking at me and would smile. The connection we had was marvelous.

Suz: did you by any chance look at the test results I forwarded to you?

Lee: the fungitell test was normal. Mid range. Not high or low. It's a test for an invasive fungal infection and you're normal

Suz: so its bacterial then?

Lee: I don't think it means that. It means that what they tested for was normal

I shared my ignorance as if I was a licensed physician.

Lee: Doctor thinks it's the TB cousin

Lee: They are taking a two-prong approach. 1 they are deciding which meds to give you for the TB cousin. And he thinks the steroid is working. Told nurse to keep it coming.

Suz: getting a little jittery from steroid I think

Lee: 2 you do the treatments which help the lungs to clear up and function properly. He said it's so important. He said there's no medicine that can take place of the breathing exercises

Suzanne texted me a photo of the cartoons I drew for her, now pinned on the nurses' corkboard. At a college part-time job at the Stars Hall of Fame wax museum, a professional artist trained me to draw caricatures. Looking back at her television, I saw players were scrambling.

Lee: fumble? Army recovered?

Suz: Not paying attention sorry. I went down the ig [Instagram] rabbit hole

I texted a picture of Charlie Brown and Snoopy standing next to his doghouse and the tiny Christmas tree. *The Charlie Brown Christmas* was our favorite Christmas show.

Suz: Hey CB [Charlie Brown]

Army scored a touchdown in the game.

Lee: Go Army

I was doing nothing but being there for Suzanne and that was everything to her—and it was the same for me. Always together. Suzanne was struggling to regain her health for the first time in her life.

Lee: You're doing the hard part

I was so proud of Suzanne as I gazed through the glass at her. The hall was dark, and she could no longer see me.

Suz: You're doing the hard part,
mine just different

She was right. We were in this together; come what may, we always stood together.

Lee: It's a team. Divide and conquer

That was one of her favorite sayings. We did tasks as a couple, but sometimes it was better to do them separately, divide, and complete the task, conquer.

Suz: Always

Lee: Always

"Always" was another key word in our relationship. It was in our marriage vows, in our hearts, and in our daily thoughts. We would always love each other, trust Jesus, be together, and make each other first in our lives. That's a really good word—always. It was a promise and a restatement of love every time we spoke it to each other.

When I got home, I put the Army-Navy game on the television so we could keep track together, even if far apart. By that time, it was near the end of the game, only a few minutes left to play. Navy was winning. Then the Army kicked a field goal.

Lee: T I E D

Suz: Missed that, I was on the potty

Lee: Army kicked a field goal to tie.
2 min to go

Suz: Dang down to the wire

The game ended in a tie. The Navy was favored to win, largely due to the Army's weak ground game. After a short break, the game started overtime play. Army scored a touchdown on its first play in overtime. The cadets went absolutely wild in the stands! The ball went to Navy, who scored a touchdown after a few plays. The game tied again as the clock hit zero. A second overtime would be played.

On its first possession, the Navy advanced rapidly, nearing the end zone. Army forced a fumble and recovered. Several running plays put Army within field goal distance. They won on a field goal with seconds remaining on the clock.

Suz: Great game

She would always state that it didn't really matter what team won because all those kids won. All those kids would be in uniform in a few months. On ships, on the ground, and in the air around the world. They would be making a difference in the world soon. It is the only game played in our country where all the players are willing to die for everyone watching the game.

Suz: tomorrow can you bring me a pair of shorts, navy shorts tight stretchy, maybe in 1st or 2nd drawer on left side of dresser

Suzanne sent me an email with things she needed when I arrived to see her tomorrow. I pulled some clothes out of her dresser, laid each one on our bed, and took photos. I texted each one to her, and she picked what she needed. Then Suzanne texted me the Vineyard Vines sale flyer to remind me to use the gift cards. It was nine-thirty p.m., and I was exhausted.

Lee: hey. Was gonna come up. But will crash with the boys

Suz: Yes please stay home. You need a chill night. Nothing going on here. Doctor Parker walked by when he was leaving and gave me a thumbs up. Next crew coming in. I'm just reading phone after the game.

Suz: Just took a breathing treatment. Getting bedside potty bc oxygen rate goes down every time I get up to go to potty. Do what ya gotta do!!

Do what you gotta do. No roadblock too great. No matter how messy the task, she pressed forward. But now Suzanne was unable to walk five feet to the small bathroom; that shocked me, and my mind raced. More prayers to Jesus for her. I could not figure out what was really going on with her health.

To occupy my mind, I logged onto the Vineyard Vines website, making selections. I took photos of each and texted them to Suzanne.

Lee: Striped polo shirt

Suz: good good

Lee: Gray quarter zip

Suz: Oh niceeeee. I hope youre using the 60% off discount code

Lee: Striped swim trunks

Suz: striped [with a thumbs up icon]

Lee: if you dig them too I'm buying

Suz: Fantastic job. Act surprised Christmas morning!

I stepped through the purchase screens and texted her a photo of the PLACE ORDER button on the screen.

Suz: Do it!

I took a photo of the "Thanks for your order!" screen and texted it to her.

Lee: BOOOM

Suz: Wooo hooooo

That expression always made me chuckle, and she said it often when she was excited.

Suz: how you feeling this evening? I hate not being able to see you! I can usually tell how you feel just by looking at you

I read her text with tears in my eyes that she could not see. We never liked to see tears in each other's eyes, as we liked being happy too much.

Lee: how you feeling?

Suz: Good. just did my lung toy. Last for the night. Think I have a new nurse. Lots of drama down the hall. Nurse said earlier today her other patient is screaming down the hall

That comment gave me a cold chill to think Suzanne had to hear that while trying to recover.

Suz: Bc soon I'll need cough med before I go to be

She paused in her testing as a nurse walked through the vestibule into her room.

Suz: Nurse just came in bringing cough med. He knows I am due for it. Nurse said I get another steroid tonight

Before I went to bed, I texted Suzanne one more message.

Lee: I love you, see you in the morning

On my earlier visit, I had noticed that the oxygen supply was now set at 20 ml, meaning she continued to need more oxygen. The doctor started at 2 ml on Thursday and was at 10 ml by Friday. I thought, *That's similar to a road sign on a highway journey, and I need to keep watching it.*

I downloaded Suzanne's latest test results. Blood tests and CT scans were done every four hours. I taught myself what each test meant and the expected test results. All week, her results continued to be normal. Only one test was elevated, almost "off the chart"; the immunoglobulin E (IgE) antibodies were extremely high. The normal reading for IgE is 0.0 – 100.0, and she was at 1,3856.00.

These antibodies are proteins that the body's immune system produces in response to allergens. If there is an allergen, the body produces more IgE in response to that allergen. I had asked the doctor about the IgE, and he said it was typical of a lung infection by a virus or bacteria.

I crawled into an empty bed again, strange to sleep alone, but I couldn't really sleep. My mind was so confused about her condition. The good and bad news were at such odds. I tossed and turned, telling myself I was asleep. Light tears began to fall as I continued to pray to Jesus to help her. I trusted Him completely and knew He was in charge.

EIGHT

The Last 48 Hours
Sunday, December 11th

My cellphone chimed in the darkness. I picked up my phone and saw 6:05 a.m. in blue light.

Suz: Morning. Can you come here this AM rather than church?

Lee: Yea! on my way

I quickly shaved and got dressed, as I didn't want to miss doctors' rounds at eight-thirty a.m. We kept texting as I continued to get ready to leave.

Suz: Ty

Lee: bringing fresh clothes

Suz: Ty

Lee: pants, shorts, DRAWERS

Suz: Different doctor came in and scared me to death

Lee: whatttt

Suz: Said respirator or ventilator is next. They are giving me 100% on the mask

Reading her words shocked me. My brain began to race, searching for answers and options. I thought she was getting better, and now this news. I prayed constantly, asking for wisdom from God. Suddenly I remembered that confusion was typical in complex situations. I calmed myself and remembered God's promise to me about trusting Him, and how He loved her more than I did.

Lee: I believe it's not as bad as it sounds

Suz: Sweet nurse Megan said we aren't there yet

Needing to understand what the doctor was suggesting, I searched for "respirator" and "ventilator." The images on my phone scared me.

Lee: It's a typical treatment for highly contagious diseases

Suz: Got uplifting news yesterday and then this so I don't know what to believe

I drove too fast to the hospital as I tried to make sense of all the doctors' words and test results. As I parked and exited Suzanne's car, I wondered how I got there. The usually full parking lot was almost vacant. A light breeze rustled the leaves in the tall pine trees around the hospital.

I pressed the lit phone button on the wall to gain access to the ICU, and the nurse on duty recognized me immediately, opening the automatic doors. I waved to her as Suzanne's doctor was walking in the hall. He told me to join them for rounds in a few minutes. Pulled my cellphone out of my pocket to text Suzanne.

Lee: I asked him if I could go in and see you and he said yes

Suz: ok good

Lee: May take an hour as they have to finish rounds

Suz: ok

Lee: was praying last night. And this kept popping into my mind. GOD told me "I will return her to you. You have to trust me". And when it hit my brain, all anxiety disappeared.

Suz: That's good, I'm working on trust

Lee: I know it's hard

She texted me a screenshot of a story written by a mom whose twenty-one-day-old son suffered cardiac arrest from a respiratory virus complication. It was the darkest day of her life. A Christmas tree gift served as a reminder that the good news of Jesus still burns bright. In the middle of the night, God sent his Son as a gift. The great joy of Jesus shattered the darkness of being separated from God. I read the story with tears in my eyes.

Lee: That's it. That's it. You will have a story to praise Jesus when you get home. I deeply deeply believe this. All my anxiety is gone. For me, I had to move from 'fear to faith' that solidified in me last night

Suz: I'm trying

My heart broke in reading her text. I knew Suzanne was scared, and I was scared too. Something wasn't right about her progress, or lack of it.

Lee: Jesus knows

Suz: Yes

Her texts were brief because she was so uneasy. The expression on her face told me what I didn't want to know. I was helpless; the only thing I could do was pray and trust Jesus, nothing more.

Lee: So grab that, hold it close, trust Jesus

Suz: Trying

Lee: we have believed [in Jesus] most of our lives. Now we get to see Him work

The group of doctors approached her room soon after, starting morning rounds in the empty, dimly lit, quiet hallway. We stood outside her room. All the doctors and nurses glanced at me briefly, none smiling. The older doctor wearing glasses led the discussion.

"Mrs. Carrick, admitted on Wednesday with pneumonia."

Many medical terms were used to explain her condition, none of which I understood. Her doctor appeared gray and didn't look at me like usual. The older doctor paused, then peered over his large glasses directly at me.

"She's not getting better."

Turning his laptop around, he showed me her latest CT scan. I recognized the right lung obscured by the pneumonia only because it was similar to Wednesday afternoon's scan. The doctors continued to discuss her case, but all I could hear was, "She's not getting better."

Then they mentioned the next patient, moving through the hall, and I left the ICU without a specific destination to clear my head.

After several minutes, I returned to the ICU. Suzanne's negative-pressure room was wide open. My heart soared as I cautiously entered. Sitting in bed with a big smile behind her oxygen mask, Suzanne waved me to come closer. I assumed they had identified the cause of the pneumonia and no longer needed the isolation. I forgot, or wanted to forget, the doctor telling me, "She's not getting better." I could not accept that statement. It wasn't faith; it was my humanity talking.

Suzanne spoke to me in person for the first time in four days. "I'll be going home in a couple of days."

I missed hearing her voice; it was a song to my heart. Holding her hand, my eyes scanned the medical monitoring equipment. The oxygen supply was at 20 ml. At the top of the monitor, her heartbeat and temperature were normal. At the bottom, the pulse oximeter fluctuated between 94% and 96%, not the target of 96% to 99%. It's the single metric I watched constantly but never mentioned to anyone. It was my key road sign on this part of the journey in our life adventure.

Our small talk continued. It didn't matter what we talked about; it was comforting to hear Suzanne's voice and bask in the banter. She ate some soup last night and liked the crushed ice with tea. Nurses were good to her, checked on her often, and sometimes chatted with her. She loved them. And they were learning to love her as well.

Her warm hands in mine sent the familiar warm glow across my body. Something about her physical touch resonated with me. It was so simple, yet communicated so much to me.

***

Promptly at nine a.m., Dr. Parker walked into her room. His usual slight smile was gone, and he was gray. His eyes darted between Suzanne and the floor. Slowly sitting in a chair, he made eye with me.

"Mrs. Carrick, I don't know how to tell you this. Except for your lungs, you are in perfect health. Your heart, your liver, your weight, and your blood pressure are perfect. You never smoked or drank alcohol. You always lived right. You did everything right. We are not one hundred percent sure, but we think it's lung cancer. Stage 4. It's a very rare, very aggressive cancer. It's a monster. It has doubled in size since we admitted you to the hospital on Wednesday evening. And it will continue to double on an exponential scale."

My mind heard what he was saying, but I could not comprehend it all.

He continued, "It only attacks very healthy people. We don't know why; I have seen this before. We have been doing tests all week. We did full-body scans, and the cancer is everywhere." He described all the places the cancer spread, and I could not keep track.

"Because you are in perfect health, I give you one to two months to live."

Suzanne whispered under her breath, "This is a nightmare." She wept.

My heart broke. *One to two months* burned inside my brain. *That means January or February. How could that be? What was going on here?*

The doctor continued, "I need to do more tests to see what your options are. I know you want to go home, but I don't know if you can. You're taking the maximum amount of oxygen now in the hospital. We can't provide that level of oxygen to you in an ambulance. You would not survive the trip home, even though it's only seven miles away."

My brain pounded as I thought, *How could this get any worse? She may not be able to go home? What did that mean?*

"Ask your kids to be here at four p.m. to tell them. I'll be here to answer any questions they have. Don't tell them unless I am with you." He shifted his focus. "I want you to be selfish with your time. I want you to do what you want. Spend this time with your family."

My brain raced, and I could not hear anymore. I held Suzanne and wept.

The next several minutes are still a blur. Total disbelief. We expected her to go home in a couple of days; now she might have to stay in the hospital and would die in one to two months. I could not process all of this.

Inside, I begged for help from Jesus.

We sat together on her bed, holding hands. I don't remember what we talked about. I told her how much I loved her. My head continued to spin: I'm the man, I'm the husband, I should know what to do, what to say in this situation. I was completely lost.

But she wasn't.

Suddenly, Suzanne spoke in a calm and determined manner, "I've had such a full life, a good life. I have no regrets. I wouldn't change a thing."

She accepted what I could not with great courage. I was stunned at her ability to process the doctor's news so quickly. To accept the fact that she was dying. This woman, whom I had known for the last forty-eight years, continued to amaze me. She always had such strong faith and conviction. This news devastated me.

It was true—she was dying. But her words, "I have no regrets," held fast in my mind.

Despite the chaos in my brain, those words made it all stop. How could she have that level of comprehension in parallel with knowing she was dying? But she did. She was confident. She was broken-hearted, but she was sure.

I looked at her in amazement. I was always so proud of her. Always respected her. And this was a whole new level of understanding and appreciation for who Suzanne was. I was blessed to be with her, and there was no place I would've rather been at that time.

The situation drew me closer to her, so I never had the desire to run away. I have always been and would always be by her side. The only regret I held was that Suzanne would be leaving me so much sooner than expected. Decades sooner. I knew this to be true in my mind, but my heart could not comprehend it.

Several minutes passed as we continued to hold hands in silence. Suddenly, Suzanne began weeping. She paused and asked me if she was good enough to go to Heaven.

She said, "I've sinned in my life."

Having known her for the last forty-eight years, I knew by the world's standards she was a good person. She walked the narrow path all her life; her love held me on the path with her. A lifelong rule-follower, Suzanne never got a speeding ticket but loved laughing at me when I did.

Suzanne's question surprised me because we both accepted Jesus as our Lord and Savior in the Easter season of 1978. We remained true followers of Jesus since that day. Then I saw her face, and I understood.

I saw fear in her eyes as she faced the biggest unknown of her life, the same as all of us will.

I responded, "You know better than that. You accepted Jesus in 1978. He died for your sins. He saved your soul. He will greet you in Heaven."

Those words came straight from Jesus through me to her; I didn't even have to think. Jesus put confidence in my voice, too. Pools of tears filled her bright blue-green eyes, and she nodded her head yes. It was almost too much for me to handle, so I prayed to Jesus for strength. And He delivered.

She then asked about Heaven, which told me she knew her destination for eternity. "Tell me what it's like."

I immediately recalled a discussion from my weekly men's group that used the *Foundations of Faith* guide, also known as the Purple Book.

"This won't be exactly scriptural, but the guys and I discussed this a couple of weeks ago. I envision you meeting Jesus and being judged.

"Before, you will be the Book of Life, which had all your sins. As Jesus touches the first one, He'll smile and say, 'I forgive you, I love you,' and that first sin will disappear from the page. He'll touch every single sin, and each one will disappear. They'll no longer exist; there is no shame or sorrow in Heaven. He will forgive all your sins and welcome you into Heaven."

Those words, too, came straight from Jesus for her. I was grateful for the Purple Book class that Nelson and Stan led.

She looked at me and smiled, nodding her head. Fewer tears, less fear.

Suzanne quietly asked to play her favorite song, "I Can Only Imagine". Sitting on the side of her bed as the music played on my cellphone, she started to sing softly. As the words floated across the room, she raised her head, continuing to sing. As she looked skyward, I could no longer hear her voice. I believe Jesus lifted her head, comforting her, as she was singing. I wept; He loves her more than I do. When the song ended, she was smiling softly. All the fear was gone, never to return, and she lay back and rested. Peace filled the room; only Jesus could make that happen.

Not sure how much time passed. Maybe thirty minutes, but likely less than an hour. Suddenly, she sat up. Suzanne turned sideways and hung her legs over the bed. I was sitting in the chair next to her bed. She was slightly higher than me with a stern expression. The kind your elementary teacher would give you when you're in trouble.

"You are not going to crawl into a hole and die on me! You have to take care of the kids, take care of the dogs, Henry," she said in a clear, strong tone.

For years, we believed that when one of us died, the other would die of heartbreak within six months. It was romantic at the time, like *The Notebook*, but no longer. For God controls the number of our days.

God started the stopwatch for our life together on Valentine's Day in 1974. And now it appeared He was going to click the stopwatch and end our earthly relationship sooner than expected. But there was no stopwatch for her in eternity. Quickly, my mind transported me back to our early days together in high school. It could be fifty years ago and yesterday all at once.

Suzanne knew exactly what was happening but never said a single word about her condition. Immediately, she focused on the people she loved. Thinking back, I am still amazed at her strength and endless love. But not surprised, as that was her nature—never focused on herself, only on others.

Still stern, Suzanne's eyes filled with tears, her voice broke. "You need to remarry. You are a companion guy. You need to be married. I want you to get remarried. You won't make it alone."

I choked and told her I could never do that.

Ignoring me, this time louder, she said, "YOU NEED TO LISTEN TO ME! I want you to remarry."

I put all my treasure in Suzanne through high school, college, military duty, kids, and cross-country moves. We experienced much over the last forty-eight years, but this was the most significant statement of love she ever said to me. Her love for me went beyond my understanding as she focused on my future, including with another woman. And she knew she was the only woman I ever loved.

At this point, I had the presence of mind to get my cellphone out of my pocket and start taking notes as she talked. She continued giving me directions for what was to come.

"I don't want the kids driving by the funeral home I will be at. Take me to this funeral home," and she showed me a web page photo of Stuhr Funeral Home she saved on her cellphone. A big red circle was drawn around the photo.

"Take care of Henry," her beloved miniature schnauzer.

"Do what you want with the house. But if you move, buy a small house in Dunes West. Not a fixer-upper, but one that is in great shape. Don't do a remodel again. And it has to have a pool. You need a pool. Do you hear me? A pool!"

At her insistence, we built our first pool when we moved to Charleston, something she had always wanted for me but could not afford. The first time I jumped in our swimming pool, she had a big smile and tears in her eyes saying, "That makes my heart sing, Lee."

"For my funeral, I want good Seacoast music. I want "I Can Only Imagine[1]," by MercyMe. And Cody Carnes and Kari Jobe's "The Blessing[2]." It must be a celebration. Do it in the chapel. Don't spend a lot of money on a casket, something decent. Bury me in the navy-blue dress in my closet. Make sure I don't have any gray hair showing."

I typed notes on my cellphone as she spoke. She knew I would have to make these decisions while being devastated, so she made them for me.

Suzanne always thought of others before herself. "Cancel my hair appointment with Heather. She shouldn't lose money because I miss my appointment next week."

"Cancel the cabin at Fort Wilderness, don't lose any money." She and Betsy did a girls' trip to Disney World each fall.

"Donate all my clothes to Seacoast. Donate all my scrapbook stuff to the seniors. I love that [Seacoast] church."

Closing her eyes, Suzanne lay back on the hospital bed, still and quiet. I checked the Telemonitor for her oxygen reading: 92%.

While she slept, I walked into the hall. The nurses looked at me, most with tears in their eyes. Surely, they knew hours, if not days, before I did, but I wondered when they first heard her diagnosis. They dreaded this moment almost as much as I did. These nurses were hurting over a woman they'd met five days ago. These women and men were special, unique, and my respect for them soared to Heaven.

Around noon, I called Matt and Betsy to ask them to visit their mom at the hospital. The cellphone calls were brief with no details, but they could sense bad news. I returned to her room; Suzanne was strong that afternoon. Ever since Jesus lifted her head and comforted her, she was totally focused on what needed to be done next. I didn't see her cry or worry; she was absorbed in her thoughts.

The oxygen flow was increased from 20 to 30 milliliters; oxygen saturation was in the low nineties. My mind assessed what was occurring, but my heart refused to accept it. My mind was searching for options, especially converting our living room into a hospital room so at least she could be home. I thought about how to care for her for the next couple of months, realizing I needed to get some help.

Matt arrived at about three p.m., with a worried look when I met him in the hospital lobby. He asked me what was going on. I told him to talk to his mom one on one.

"What's up?"

"Talk to Mom."

They talked inside the ICU room while I waited outside. Betsy arrived soon after, deep concern on her face. She and Suzanne talked alone in the room after Matt was done. I'm not sure what Suzanne told Matt and Betsy, but likely she told them how much she loved them, how proud she was of them, and encouraged them to have a good life. And keep an eye on Dad, their crazy dad.

After Suzanne talked to Matt and Betsy, we gathered together around her bed as a family. It's still foggy what we talked about. As they talked, I mentally planned, preparing our house for her arrival. My mind flipped back and forth from planning to disbelief.

At five p.m., Dr. Parker returned to her room. After I introduced him to Matt and Betsy, he started immediately with the latest medical news. He said that they had given her a different oxygen mask, allowing ten additional milliliters of oxygen to flow, and the thirty milliliters she was now receiving was the maximum. Unless they intubated her.

"Absolutely not!" Suzanne said, as that fact was in her living will.

He nodded and said that if they intubated her, she would be too weak to recover and never get off the ventilator.

Based on her condition and need for more oxygen than could be supplied, she didn't have the option of going home. She would stay at the hospital in Charleston as long as needed and be cared for as long as necessary. Hospice would be provided by her nurses to ease her transition.

Dr. Parker then stopped and started to weep, lowering his head as tears flowed. Somehow in this moment of terrible grief and sadness, Suzanne leaned forward, placing her hand on his shoulder, and said in a calm, steady voice, "It's okay Dr. Parker, it's okay. Take your time."

He raised his head and looked directly at her in total disbelief. I wondered if he was thinking, *This woman is dying; how can she be comforting me?* Stunned by her strength to comfort this man she had met him four days ago.

Only Jesus could give her this strength. Her focus was on Dr. Parker at that moment. He needed compassion, and Jesus gave it to him through Suzanne.

Words came to me, and I said out loud, "It's okay to be human, Dr. Parker."

He looked at me with tears in his eyes and said, "Doctors aren't allowed to be human. People don't believe that."

My heart broke again; I never knew the burden doctors carry. He must have known yesterday and was able to hide his dismay when he was in her room the day before. I could tell he truly liked Suzanne; perhaps it was respect for how she was handling her time in the hospital.

I suspect we were in a state of shock as we processed this new information. The term "hospice" rang in my head like a fire alarm. My mother was eighty-three when she started hospice about four years ago, so I knew exactly what hospice was and how the process worked. A part of my brain fought the knowledge. *This can't be my wife he is talking about.* The fog came back as my mind raced, searching for answers on what to do next. I assured myself that we had at least a couple of months with her, or more. No need to worry about all those details today.

All I remember is Suzanne talking to the kids. Betsy sat beside her on the bed while Matt stood next to her. She discussed how she felt, told them she loved them. They told her what was new at work, some random talk to fill the space. No one was sure what to say but knew they didn't want it to be quiet in the room. Quiet would allow all of us to think, and none of us wanted to do that.

Again, I was shocked by how confident and calm Suzanne was at that time. She calmly answered their questions and assured them it would all be good. Her positive demeanor put us all at ease. I didn't see her break down and cry again, and she never complained about the diagnosis. She accepted it and told them Jesus was in charge.

Suzanne was the strongest, most positive person I ever knew. What I was witnessing was on a different level of faith. Jesus gave her the strength to help the most important things in the world to her, Matt, and Betsy. Spending over forty years in the defense world, I worked with brave, combat-proven men and women. But I wasn't sure they could handle a situation like she was. Silently, I thanked Jesus for her and praised Him for the last forty-eight years with her.

The dialog slowed, because none of us were sure what to say. Sensing they needed time alone to process this, Suzanne suggested the kids go home. They reluctantly agreed and looked at me.

"I'll stay with her; you guys go home."

They coordinated on take-out for dinner on the way home. Suzanne closed her eyes and rested. I sat in the chair next to her, holding her hand, a simple act but often memorable now. Such as the first time I nervously held her hand in high school, at the altar, and in operating rooms when our kids were born. It was an honor to be there with Suzanne, and I would be nowhere else.

The lighting in the room was dim, and the hallway was dark. The continual flow of oxygen that was keeping her alive and the frequent beeps of the medical equipment kept us company. The machines cast a multicolored glow across the floor.

In my mind, I played our life together over and over. My conscious mind would interrupt our life movie, and I started planning mentally for what we would need to do for the next couple of months while she was in the hospital. And what to do when hospice would begin at some point. The change was inevitable, but I refused to accept it. I claimed Suzanne would be healed and believed it would happen because I wanted it so desperately.

The Lee and Suzanne story spun through my mind, and I remembered more events the longer I thought. As my movie reel played, I thanked Jesus, realizing I had one to two months with her, maybe a bit more. She rested peacefully now; the pain and fear on her beautiful face were foreign. I was glad those emotions were gone while she slept, and I thanked Him for all her love, all the laughs, all the smiles she gave me. *Forty-eight years is a long time*, I thought and laughed at myself. Of course, that had been a long time, but it didn't seem like it; it never did. Life with Suzanne was so effortless. So easy, so delightful. My mind continued to switch between topics.

Remembering her words, "I have no regrets; I wouldn't change a thing," blessed me. Her words summarized the last forty-eight years in a package with a bow.

When I proposed to her, I said, "I may never have any money, but I will always love you, and we'll always have fun." We kept our simple, timeless wedding vows so critical in a relationship. A smile crept across my face, breaking the stream of tears that continued to flow. I, too, had no regrets and would not change a thing in our lives. Replaying our life together brought joy and escape from the harsh reality, even though only for a few minutes.

Never one to wait patiently, I strolled through the hospital halls before midnight, peering outside. A handful of empty cars dotted the parking lot. Constantly thinking of ways to help Suzanne, I realized seeing her beloved miniature schnauzer would be a boost. I quickly turned and headed for the elevator, devising a plan. I found an open back exit door. Closing it softly to prevent locking, I ran to the front parking lot. I texted Betsy, asking her to get Henry ready to visit Suzanne. She may have thought I was crazy, but Henry was ready to roll when I arrived.

Traffic late on a Sunday night was nonexistent, and we arrived at the hospital quickly. Once the car was parked, we walked Henry to the rear exit door. My quick rush of fear passed, realizing all the police could do was tell me to take the dog home. The elevator doors opened, revealing no passengers in the elevator car until we slid in silently. A ding sounded when the elevator stopped at the second floor and for the first time in his life, Henry did not bark at the sound.

We peered cautiously around the elevator doors like burglars to confirm the nurse's station was empty. I quietly walked to smuggle Henry into her room; glad it was the closest to the doors, Room #1.

Suzanne's face brightened as she reached for Henry, as she was awake by then. I lifted him over the side of her bed past the many pieces of hospital equipment. She hugged him tight, but he was uneasy. He refused to relax nor look at her. She remarked, "Ohhh, he doesn't recognize me."

Betsy and I looked at each other, wondering what that meant. After a few minutes, Henry got more agitated, and Suzanne asked us to take him back home.

I returned to the hospital via the main entrance, partly expecting Security to question me about the dog. Once back in her room, I checked the oxygen saturation reading, 92%, which required a 911 call. The oxygen flowed at 30 milliliters with a loud hiss. She received the maximum amount of oxygen, but her lungs could not process it efficiently. My heart sank. It was one-thirty a.m., and she was sleeping again. Still in disbelief of the situation. Still comforted by the love of Jesus.

Love was the only thing keeping me going forward.

Suddenly, Suzanne woke up, sat up, looked at me, and said harshly, "GO HOME!" and lay back down.

It shocked me because she never spoke to me like that, and then I realized she was worried about me and knew that was the only way to get me to go home.

NINE

Love Prevails
Monday, December 12th

Despite the previous day's diagnosis, Suzanne continued the painful lung treatments. Always a fighter. As I waited in the hall, the doctors made morning rounds but did not stop at her room. Her doctor left the group and stood next to me, watching her.

"She is amazing," Dr. Parker said softly, glancing at me with tears in his eyes.

As difficult as the situation was, I was so proud to be there. She was my wife, the love of my life. Despite the tears, I stood tall and firm. Suzanne needed me now like never before. Refusing to falter, I vowed to never let her down. My confidence built as I mentally prepared for the weeks to come. This was a different side of love for the first time. Meanwhile, the nurses walked by uncomfortably and looked at Suzanne in her room, and then at me. One by one, they paused to talk with me.

They were all heartbroken, with tears in their eyes, commenting that Suzanne was the kindest and nicest patient they had ever had. Her faith and peace were unusual. Despite the doctor's words yesterday morning, she continued to be so kind to them and never complained. The nurses witnessed a different kind of story unfold—a woman who loved Jesus all her life and accepted His decision for her life on earth. She knew He would greet her in Heaven, forty-four years after she surrendered her life to Him. That decision led to a blessed life, two wonderful children, lovely friends, and good health. She was always content in life, and I was proud of her.

As Suzanne continued the lung treatments, I was amazed at her strength and determination. She switched between an earthly and heavenly perspective often. She knew her time here was short but still fought to stay with us as long as possible. I wondered how many weeks we would be with her here, but I feared it would be hard for her with so much pain and discomfort. As I looked into her room that day, I again wondered if Jesus had sent an angel to care for her. Was He in the room watching over her, protecting her, and conveying God's messages to her?

I never saw any indication this was occurring, but in my heart, I believed it to be true. An indescribable peace permeated the room. We knew the diagnosis had become a fact we accepted and didn't dwell on. But I know that peace was there thanks to Jesus.

Matt, Betsy, and Suzanne's brother, Steve, arrived around eleven a.m. The kids were smiling, and I was proud of them. They would be strong for Suzanne and make her day brighter. They ignored the hospital's noisy machines, the frequent equipment beeps, and the hiss of the oxygen supply. Suzanne beamed with joy when she saw them. Mostly, it was like a visit to a nice lady in the hospital who was feeling better and would be released to go home soon.

Instinctively, the kids told funny family stories to soften the mood. Laughter was welcomed, which amplified the peace in the room. When the nurses checked on her throughout the day, they were surprised to witness our laughter.

Her nurse delivered iced tea and soup using the food in the nurses' breakroom. Suzanne smiled when she noticed the small nuggets of ice in her Styrofoam cup. As we continued to tell stories and laugh, I thought again about the wonderful life Suzanne gave us. She made everything beautiful. We took turns sitting in the chair beside her bed and took photos, unaware it would be the last time we would take photos with her. Big smiles were on her face as she posed with Matt, then Betsy. On my turn, she gave me "My Smile." Her eyes displayed love with a wide grin under her oxygen mask. Then, in classic Suzanne style, she flashed a "peace sign" as the picture was taken.

The hand gesture initially was a "V for Victory" sign, started by Winston Churchill during World War II to garner optimism for Britain. The sixties had changed that hand gesture's meaning, but no matter, it made us all laugh. And indeed, it was victory. Victory over death.

As we laughed, I marveled at her optimism and strength. I glanced at the monitor and noticed the numbers had not improved. I continued to pray for her healing and expected at some point to see the numbers improve. As I watched her interact with the kids, I remember thinking there is no way this is humanly possible, Jesus is helping her and all of us get through this. He is always good.

As we finished taking our photos, the Kids Coast team walked into the room. These amazing ladies led the largest ministry at Seacoast Church. On a typical Sunday, they ministered to almost a thousand children; their dedication to sharing the gospel with children was remarkable. Suzanne and I were always honored to be able to support them each week in their mission. All the ladies stood in her room, with smiles on their faces. They, too, were in soldier mode.

When they walked in, Suzanne beamed with happiness, fighting back tears. She was proud of these ladies and happy they stopped by to see her. I too was glad they all came, thinking there would be plenty of time in the next few weeks for them to visit her.

They demonstrated kindness and empathy, along with smiles and hugs. Each lady kneeled beside her bed and spoke with her. I didn't hear the discussion, but I could tell it was impactful by the expression on Suzanne's face. Tears rolled down my cheeks at the sight. This was not a farewell; it was "I love you" and "we'll see each other again." Those words did not need to be spoken; the message was understood.

A few minutes later, Joel Delph, our Seacoast campus pastor, walked into the room. He was also in soldier mode, as well, as he lit up the room speaking to everyone, then asked Suzanne, "How ya doing?"

Struggling to talk with her oxygen mask on, Suzanne said, "I never thought Seacoast could get any better, then you showed up."

I saw the look on Joel's face, and he almost broke. She touched his heart with a simple statement and smile. Joel's smile returned from a brief show of emotion, then he was back in soldier mode; he had a job to do. He was here now for his friend and my wife, who was one of over six thousand members. He recited the Lord's Prayer in Luke 11:1-4 and the importance of our prayers seeking God's intervention in Luke 11:5-13.

Joel added, "We have two miracles in front of us, the miracle of Heaven and the miracle of healing. We want to live a life surrendered to God's will to be done, because He is the only one in the room not surprised by any of this. It's perfectly good and healthy for us to pray, believing in the gift of healing." And that's what we did. He asked us to think about the *peace that surpasses all understanding.*

Anointing her head with oil, he prayed for Jesus to heal Suzanne. I wanted it to happen, as did she, saying yesterday, "I have so much left to do."

I glanced at her oxygen monitor of 92% as usual. As Joel and the group continued to pray, the monitor slowly climbed to 95%, the highest reading of her stay. Then quickly progressed to 98%.

My mind attempted to comprehend what occurred. The monitor climbed to 100%, which wasn't possible according to the nurses. I watched the monitor in disbelief as Joel continued to pray. At that point, I could no longer hear Joel; I was completely focused on the road sign reading for Suzanne's oxygen level, which reached 100%. My mind was racing, not sure what to do or say next. Joel finished praying, and we all started to talk.

Several minutes passed before Joel and the Kids Coast team said goodbye and departed. I was so thankful for all of them coming by. My eyes darted back to the monitor, which read 98%.

The nurse came in to conduct her rounds, so we moved the extra chairs out of the room. When I returned, the monitor was at 92%. I have no evidence, but I will always believe that as Joel and the Kids Coast team prayed, the Holy Spirit filled the room at that time. No other explanation was possible to drive her oxygen saturation to 100%. A few days later, I saw Joel and told him about the change. His eyes got wide, and he uttered, "Wow."

After our friends left, we arranged the chairs around Suzanne's bed. I asked Steve to tell us about growing up with Suzanne, who was six years younger. He laughed.

"Oh, she was a pain. She was a little kid who kept bugging me. Always coming into my room. It was really bad when my friends came to the house because she would not leave us alone."

Laughter ensued as Suzanne smiled.

"I met Vince at Sunday School at College Park Methodist Church when I was twelve, and he was too," Steve continued. "We've been buddies ever since. But the worst part was that Vince had a sister the same age as Suzanne; her name was Patricia. Whenever we were at each other's house, Suzanne and Patricia would pester us like crazy. We could not make them go away."

Matt and Betsy roared. Suzanne shot him that little sister glare, and he laughed.

She turned the tables on him, taking the spiral notebook, I gave her to write messages; her need for oxygen was so high that she could barely talk at this point. With a red pen, she scribbled words on a page, then flipped the notebook around to display "VW crash."

We all laughed.

"Okay," said Steve. "Really wasn't my fault."

More laughter.

"I had just gotten this VW bug a couple of weeks prior. Didn't really know how to drive it well. We were on Edgewater Drive [in College Park, Florida] just fooling around. Looking at girls walking down the street. Next thing I know, I hop a curb and hit a fire hydrant."

Suzanne belly laughed. He tried to defend this fifty-year-old fender bender but made us laugh all the harder.

"All right, all right, I give up," he said, surrendering to the laughter.

His little sister began scribbling in her notebook again, enjoying the revenge on big brother. Turning the notebook around, we read, "2nd accident."

We howled even louder.

"Oh, okay, that's how it's gonna be, huh?" he said.

She nodded, pointing at him.

"So that wasn't my fault either," as if he were talking to his father when he was sixteen years old.

More laughter.

"Yeah, so I'm driving home and turned the corner, and there was this car. I wasn't going fast. Well, yeah. I hit it."

Laughter filled the air. Suzanne scribbled. The word "booze" was scribbled in red on the paper. Now the kids were really howling while Steve's face went pale.

"Uh … uh … yeah, maybe alcohol was involved," still trying to cover his tracks.

At this point, the kids were crying tears of laughter, and Suzanne was loving every second of it.

Steve tried to bail out, saying, "Okay, okay, let's talk about Suzanne."

Suzanne's face became stern, and she flipped him "the bird." The dreaded middle finger!

The kids shouted, "WHOAAAA!" and "WHATTTTT?" They had never seen her do that gesture, and I don't think I had either. After a brief period of silence in shock, they cackled too. Steve was loving getting her back and may have won that battle, but Suzanne was about to win the war.

As she scribbled in the spiral notebook, we all watched with great anticipation. A devious smile crossed her face as she put the pen down. She looked at Steve, still hiding her writing. Slowly, she turned the notebook around to reveal "hit a kid with car."

The kids lost it. Steve rolled his eyes and uttered, "Oh man … not that. Well, it's not exactly like that," looking at Suzanne, who was laughing, nodding.

"It really wasn't my fault."

Even more laughter erupted.

Steve laughed nervously before sharing the story. "I was driving the VW bug down the street in a friend's neighborhood. A young kid on a bike came storming out of a driveway right in front of me. I hit him with the right side. Fortunately, I was going slow. I got out of my car and checked on him. He said he was okay. I helped him get back on his bike, and I drove off."

The kids' faces were ashen as they shouted, "HIT N' RUN, Uncle Steve?!?"

He chuckled. "Yeah, I guess so. Later that afternoon, the cops knocked on my parents' door. I told them the story, and it ended okay. I didn't get in trouble," and tried to pretend like it didn't bother him.

Suzanne howled with laughter. Being the little sister all those years and holding onto the dark family secrets were finally paying off.

Steve looked at Matt. "Okay, man, I'm done," laughing. "You tell one."

Matt crossed his arms with a smile. "My favorite mom and dad story happened one morning at breakfast. We [Matt & Betsy] were still living at home. Dad was sitting at the table. Mom never liked mornings and was moving slowly. She had on a wrinkled robe, and her hair was a mess. Which was unusual because she always looked nice in the morning by the time we came down for breakfast. Mom appeared really tired and wasn't cooking.

"There were muffins on the table. Dad was sitting at the table. He put a muffin on a plate. Mom was standing by the sink between Dad and the microwave. He asked Mom if she would warm the muffin for him. She took the plate and, with this sinister look, held the plate to her mouth, exhaled on it, and handed it back to him."

Suzanne laughed heartily; she loved to tease me. We always played games on each other. She was better at it than I was because she was a cool customer, and I didn't know what was happening until it was too late.

We talked and laughed until nine-thirty p.m.; it had been a full day for Suzanne, and she loved talking with everyone who visited. Unfortunately, her condition slowly worsened, although no one could tell because she was so alert and active. She still had that playful silliness I loved so much about her. But I could tell she was tired. I suggested everyone go home and get some rest, expecting tough weeks ahead so we needed to pace ourselves.

Steve planned to fly back to Tampa and return with his wife to spend time with Suzanne. The kids would need to go back to work. I wasn't sure what to expect, but I knew I would never leave her side. We could figure it all out as it came to us. I always wanted to be with Suzanne. That was the sweetest word I knew; together.

It was almost ten p.m. when she rose from her chair and crawled into bed with a nurse's help.

"I'm tired, and I'm going to take a nap."

I tried to imagine all the things in her mind as Suzanne watched her brother and two kids hug her and walk out of her room. "Goodbye, see you tomorrow" took on a new meaning. She knew she was dying, as did I at this point. Suzanne and I knew there would be no healing on earth. She never asked, "Why me?" She never got mad at God, and I will always be convinced that Jesus met her in her time of greatest need and gave her a comfort beyond human understanding. Suzanne was the most amazing person I had ever known, and God loaned her to me to love and care for as long as He wanted. But He was her Father; she belonged to Him.

As she slept, I paced the hall; the other visitors had departed. The nurses had dimmed the hallway lights, and calm permeated the ICU. I felt comfort in the soft glow that crept from the nurses' station, through the hallway, and across Suzanne's bed. Even the dim glow of the health monitor was a comfort. I still hoped the one specific number would slowly creep from 92% to 98% and hold steady. When that happened, I would be driving her home soon. I knew the prognosis was grim, and many people, including the Seacoast leadership, prayed for her. In her simple and quiet way, Suzanne touched many lives.

I returned to the recliner next to her bed to hold her hand as she slept. She was unable to hold my hand, so I didn't let go of hers. Although holding hands was an everyday occurrence, it was always a way to say silently that "I love you." There were times when it drew a line in our hearts that we would always remember. I held her hand when I asked her to marry me. I held her hand at our wedding. I held her hand when Matt was born late in the day in a small town in Florida. I held her hand when Betsy was born early in the morning on a military base on the coast of California, and I held her hand now. Never understood how an act that was so simple and common could be so impactful. It says everything that words alone cannot communicate.

Hours passed as I lay in the recliner next to her bed, holding her hand. My mind shifted to the inevitable. She was dying, and I needed to do whatever it took to help Suzanne in her last weeks with us on earth. I knew what occurred when a person started the final steps to death. At that point in life, everything gets medical and factual. Feelings must disappear to allow me to help her anyway I could.

Her night nurse, Tammy, who Suzanne loved immediately, asked me to let her know how Suzanne was doing. I knew that nurses could tell when death is imminent. Not an exact time, but certainly when it's 24 to 48 hours away.

I told Tammy that I knew she would know when Suzanne's death was imminent. A shocked expression crossed her face. I guessed she was searching for the right thing to say, but she could tell I was serious. Her eyes were wide, and I could tell she was hurting. Tammy didn't want to think about Suzanne dying either.

Before she could respond, I rescued her and said, "It's okay, Tammy, I know. I understand. Just tell me, please."

She glanced at the floor, raised her head, and then looked at me with a nod. I will always be in awe of these remarkable women and men who serve in this capacity, as I said earlier in the book.

Back in the gold vinyl recliner, I held Suzanne's hand again. I drifted in and out of sleep, checking the monitor for a miracle. Still 92%. I awoke when Suzanne started to thrash, and I knew what was transpiring. When I found Tammy, my expression spoke before my words.

She rushed into the room, glancing at the monitor as she took Suzanne's vitals. Turning her head toward me, she said, "It's time to start the morphine." Her training kicked in as she sought approval to start hospice.

The approval returned within minutes from the hospital. All the nurses knew, but they retained their game faces and never revealed how close death was. But it didn't feel like death. Such an awful word. Too much negativity. Too much misunderstanding. Too scary. People don't talk about it and hope it will go away. I didn't want to accept it in some ways, but my heart knew it was time.

The most horrific event I could ever imagine had begun, and there was no turning back. There would be no healing, not on this earth. And I, too, was in battle mode, although I didn't get myself there mentally. I know it was Jesus comforting me and protecting me from the human impact of seeing the death of the most important person I had known in my entire life. The only person who truly knew the real me and still loved me deeply. There were no tears, no rapid heartbeat, no light-headed feeling.

Those emotions that I dreaded never appeared. I realized it and immediately knew that Jesus was carrying me through this event as He had done so many times before. I didn't even ask Him. Didn't even think to ask Him. But He knew, and He was there.

Tammy typed on the laptop behind the curtain. She clicked the mouse on the selection of "Morphine 4 mg." She moused around and selected a few more areas. Tammy then walked away on her mission to help my wife, her new friend, make the transition easier. Her precision and professionalism were mixed with love. I saw no emotion on her face as she inserted the syringe into the IV. Slowly, the plunger moved down. Within seconds, Suzanne relaxed and became calm.

Tammy looked at me and said, "That will help her."

I had no emotions other than gratitude. We were on the path; we all had a part to play. No time for emotions and self-pity. We would do whatever Suzanne needed.

The room was still and quiet again. A glow from the dimly lit hallway and the beeping of medical monitors slipped into the room.

92%.

I lay back in the recliner and held Suzanne's left hand again. The hand with her wedding band. I thought how gracious it was of the hospital to provide a comfortable vinyl chair that I could sit and recline in. I thought that I would be here for many nights to come. Maybe a few weeks. I had no idea how much time I had with her. My lifetime love.

In the meantime, I didn't really sleep and kept my hand on hers. It felt natural, and I could tell when she moved. A few times, she shifted a bit. And then she moved significantly.

I walked into the hall when this occurred. Tammy saw me. No words were spoken.

She asked for permission, and it was granted immediately. Another selection with the mouse and a click. She left the room and returned with a syringe. Again, Suzanne was calm. It had been less than four hours. Somehow, I knew the interval between requests for morphine would shorten. No one told me, but it was obvious to me her time on earth was ending soon.

TEN

Joy, Then Peace
Tuesday, December 13th

Early morning rounds led to what was happening in Suzanne's room. As Tammy conducted her proven routine, I was in the recliner, awake but groggy. In the darkened room, as Tammy checked vital signs, she scanned each of the monitors. As she tapped her laptop keyboard, I dragged myself out of the recliner, walking behind the curtain to talk to her.

She paused her routine, saying sternly, "It's gonna be five minutes, fifteen minutes, or fifteen hours: tell your family to come now."

The lack of emotion made it easier to comprehend. What we felt didn't matter; all that mattered was Suzanne.

I texted Tammy's exact words to Matt, Betsy, and Steve. I realized it would create chaos but decided it was best to use her precise wording. Death was near, and I wanted the message to be conveyed clearly, as Tammy had communicated to me. They all responded quickly.

The fact that the love of my life, my only best friend, was now in hospice care and would never wake up was a simple fact. It had the same lack of impact as noticing the hallway walls were painted beige. Both were only facts. No emotion, at least not enough to distract me from the upcoming tasks. I didn't know what events were coming, only the last one. I knew the journey would end here and start anew when Suzanne entered eternity with Jesus. I was on the final journey in our adventure, without a map or a timeline, but my goal was to proceed as God designed. Through this, I learned death is a personal event between Suzanne and her Lord. Feeling helpless, I recalled the promises from Jesus six days prior, and comfort ensued within me.

As Suzanne lay in her hospital bed, I believed Jesus comforted her, preparing her for the jump to Heaven. I wondered if angels were waiting in her room, or would they arrive at the exact instant she would transition from an earthly life to one with the Lord? Somehow, I knew it would be more than one angel. How long would it take to go from death to eternal life with Jesus? Would it be seconds, hours, or days? I did not know or even attempt to hazard a guess.

Matt and Steve arrived thirty minutes later; their faces were pale. The expression on Matt's face was new to me, a mix of fear and uncertainty. I asked them to spend time with Suzanne separately. Even though she was not conversant, she could hear their voices and feel their touch.

Steve displayed a stoic expression and carried a hardback book under his arm—he was ready for the long haul. I accepted the lead responsibility, knowing uncertainty lay before us. Emotions are strange. How could I go from an intimate time of holding my wife's hand, thinking about our life together for the last forty-eight years, and suddenly switch to being focused on an event I had never experienced, nor expected? I believed husbands die first and was now glad to be able to lead in Suzanne's time of greatest need. Life is unpredictable; I was glad I had prepared in advance as best as possible for Suzanne's transition.

Matt left her room shaken and sobbing heavily. I thought it must be difficult to see his mom without her hearty laugh. She loved to tease the kids to get a reaction and make them laugh.

Then, Steve went to see his little sister. His wife had been fighting cancer for the last ten years. I wondered if he always expected to see his wife like this, but never his little sister; that was beyond painful for him. When he came out, he said, "I never thought this would happen. Never."

He walked through the hall to collect himself. Betsy went to see her mom, as she had arrived soon after the guys did. I think she had accepted the gravity of the situation even before she saw Suzanne on Sunday afternoon. After a few minutes, Betsy asked Matt to come into the room. We stood around Suzanne's hospital bed, not sure what to do or say. I looked at the oxygen saturation monitor; the number 75% glowed in light blue in the dark room. I knew what it meant immediately.

A nurse slowly opened the door, announcing that visitors were in the ICU waiting room. Time was passing fast; it was nine a.m. We were at the point of death, and I was selfish with her time.

I asked Matt to check on the visitors. Josh Surratt, our lead pastor, and several other pastors were in the waiting room. I asked Matt to bring Josh into the ICU. As Josh and Matt walked past the ICU double doors, I saw the pain on Josh's face, and it struck me immediately how difficult his job was. I assumed he got calls like this all the time and had to show up at all hours of the day, having to know exactly what to say.

Listening to him preach for the last few years, I knew Josh was genuine and believed he was a regular guy. A humble man on a mission to serve Jesus. I thought he probably prepared for each hospital visit by praying and tailoring his words to the person and their family. I had empathy for his pain and respect for his calling.

He said hello, and I thanked him for coming. I told him we were at the point of death and wanted to talk outside the room first. Again, I thanked him for coming.

He nodded and mentioned he was praying for us this morning, and the Lord gave him Psalm 126:5. "Let those who plant with tears reap the harvest with joyful shouts."

I was not familiar with the verse and typed into my cellphone "Psalm 126 5" so I wouldn't forget. It sounded reasonable because it was about sorrow, but I did not understand the joy part. How can there be joy in her death? I didn't realize till a few hours later how prophetic that verse was. It was the first time I heard "joy" associated with Suzanne's passing. I didn't understand it initially, but soon I would.

He said all the Seacoast church staff were praying for her. I heard his words, but I didn't really understand. I assumed Suzanne was on a prayer list with others, and that was the right thing to do. I would later learn he was completely accurate. The staff learned of Suzanne's situation the night of the Dream Team Appreciation event. They knew Suzanne and appreciated her quiet and consistent dedication. None of them could have predicted the events of the next six days.

Realizing Josh was concerned, his authenticity and humble nature touched my heart. I told him we appreciated Seacoast and that the Kids Coast team was wonderful. He smiled when I told him Suzanne and I watched the Dream Team celebration on my cellphone and thanked him for the outstanding technology the church provided.

He smiled briefly and spoke from his heart, "I came here to comfort you all, and now I am the one getting the blessing. That never happens." He looked at me somewhat in disbelief. I wasn't sure what to say next as his words surprised me, and, in some ways, they didn't.

Pastors, maybe like doctors, are expected to have all the right words at the most difficult of times. Instead, they are expected to know all the answers to any questions immediately and to point people in the right direction. They, too, are not allowed to be human sometimes but are expected to quickly and succinctly answer all the "why" questions when often only God knows why. And often only God could comprehend why His multi-generational plan is unveiled every day. While we know He wants the best for us, it's likely impossible for us humans to comprehend. I think that's what faith is all about. Not knowing all the answers but trusting the God who does.

My heart broke as I watched Josh turn and walk out of the ICU. Could there be a more challenging job on earth than being a pastor? He dealt in a world more important than life on earth. His quest is to guide people to live a fulfilling life on earth. To know and serve a loving God. His battle against the declining culture required daily engagement, and he knew that our time on this earth, while short, is absolutely critical to our long-term existence in eternity. I believe it's one of those jobs that many people want the title and prestige, but not the work to get there or the sacrifices required to sustain the role.

Soon Matt walked out of the ICU with him and to the waiting room. I walked back into Suzanne's room.

The ICU nurses change shifts at 7 a.m. and 7 p.m. It had been about two and a half hours since Suzanne's nurse had come on duty. Seeing Josh depart, a new nurse entered the room. She displayed a depth of confidence; I knew immediately she was in charge and knew her tasks. Her scrubs were pressed, and her hair was perfect. She didn't smile and concentrated only on Suzanne.

She introduced herself as Christine and said she would be taking care of Suzanne today as she straightened the bed linen. Quickly and expertly, she checked the monitors, ensuring all the equipment was operating correctly. She moved Suzanne slightly to one side to make her more comfortable. Suzanne could not tell her, but Christine knew how to position her. She adjusted Suzanne's oxygen mask as well.

Christine asked questions, and I introduced myself and my daughter, Betsy, who was in the room with me. Steve was in the waiting room.

I knew the only things foreign to her in the room were Betsy and me. She moved to the hospital laptop, typing furiously. I realized that after the shift overlap with Tammy, Christine knew exactly what was going on and determined what and how to do Suzanne's care moving forward. The only variable was these new people in the room she worked in every week. We were now in Christine's room; this was where she applied her skills and met her calling. She treated us as guests and Suzanne as the guest of honor.

Matt returned to the room. In my heart, I knew I would stay with Suzanne as long as it took to see her off to Heaven. I would never leave her side. I didn't know if it would be a few hours or a few days, but I assumed it was a week or less. I also knew what a body goes through in the last stages of death, and it can be unnerving. I did not want my two kids' last memories of their mother to be traumatic. This was hard enough, being only forty-eight hours since they heard the news.

I thought, *Wait ... we have one to two months with her.* When the doctor first said he was giving her one to two months, the time seemed incredibly short. Now it was incredibly long, and we would spend all of it in the ICU.

I spoke first, "I'm staying with her to the end. When a person dies, it can be traumatic. Sometimes terrible things occur." I elected to omit any details and stopped. "Please do what you want, stay or go. Either is fine. Do what is best for you."

Matt, who was visibly shaken, said that he needed to go home and pray. With heavy sobs, he turned, brushed the privacy curtains aside, and walked into the hallway.

Betsy lifted her purse and started to walk away. She paused and looked at Suzanne. After a few minutes of silence, she said, "I'm going to stay awhile," and came back into the room.

Christine watched this unfold as she was calculating the next steps and cautiously analyzing the relationship. And I was analyzing her. Seeing her stoic and busy, I thought she may have lost all her compassion to execute her duties. It was immediately apparent that Christine took her job seriously, and the only thing that mattered was Suzanne. Somehow, I knew she would protect Suzanne even if she had to throw us all out of the building. I started to understand her a bit, and I was impressed. She was a veteran who knew the battle plan and was executing it efficiently.

The hospice routine was being used, and requests for approval to administer morphine were no longer required. While Betsy and I focused our attention on ensuring Suzanne knew we were there, Christine was watching the vitals. I noticed that the morphine shots were more frequent. Suzanne displayed no reaction, continuing to rest peacefully.

Clearly, Christine heard Betsy and me talking as we held Suzanne's hands. She heard us speak about our faith and asked if I wanted to listen to some gospel music. I appreciated her suggestion and agreed, pulling out my cellphone. My fingers struggled to press the correct buttons in a task that I could typically do without thinking. Praise and worship music filled the room once I found the right buttons.

Christine left and quickly returned with a small Bluetooth speaker. "Connect it, and it will sound better."

How did she have the capacity to think about us? She wanted her room to be comforting for all her guests. I thanked Jesus for putting Christine on duty that day. The music played softly in the background, providing a wonderful backdrop, washing out the hiss of the oxygen feed and equipment beeps.

The alarms on Suzanne's monitor grew more frequent. Christine moved toward the monitor and turned the alarm volume lower to spare us the constant reminder of Suzanne's condition worsening. I realized the beeps were not important now, not like a few days ago. Those beeps were alerts for the nurses to stop and take immediate action. But now they were like road signs as I travelled further on this journey that now had an end ahead. There would be more beeps, but they didn't matter anymore.

"She can hear everything you are saying. She can feel you holding her hands. Keep talking to her," Christine said with complete confidence and conviction.

I looked at Christine in awe. I didn't know that was the case, and it comforted me to hear it. I was so happy to know that Suzanne knew we were there and that we loved her so much. Yes, Suzanne was still aware. She knew I was there and knew Betsy was there. And I believe she was smiling inside. If she could have, Suzanne would have told us both to leave earlier in the morning. And now Suzanne was probably glad she couldn't.

Warm sunlight flowed into Christine's room as the sun continued to rise. Seemed like it was dark outside only a few minutes ago. Time stood still and sped by all at the same time. Through the window, I saw the beautiful light blue sky so typical in South Carolina. Even in December.

Suzanne told me years ago that the Lord guided her to the Charleston area; this was the place for us to live. Jesus knew this day was coming, and I am glad I didn't.

I used to think I wanted to know what was coming in my future. Now I know it is a blessing to live each day to its fullest and let the Lord handle the future. As I held Suzanne's hand, I looked at her face. So many wonderful memories. No man ever loved a woman more than I loved her. I will always be eternally grateful to her. I thanked the Lord for protecting my heart now, keeping my emotions at bay, and allowing me to remain in battle mode.

"Dad."

I looked at Betsy, who was sitting next to Suzanne, holding her right hand.

"You're going to have a good life. It will be a different life, but still a good life. You will do different things. Not a better life than with Mommy, but a good life."

I was stunned. Her words went straight into my soul, and I knew the Lord was guiding her message. Betsy's words changed my life from that point forward. She gave me a glimpse of my new life. This was the end of a life I had loved for the last forty-eight years, and now I was at the precipice of a new life for me. I knew immediately in my heart and soul she was correct.

"You won't even recognize how good it will be. You won't recognize yourself. You'll be a different person, not a better person, just different."

I was stunned at the clarity of her words and conviction in her voice. It's as if someone had shown her the future, and she knew I needed a light to guide me through. I thank Jesus for giving her those words for me. They were so powerful to come from her, the daughter I loved and respected so much. To hear a human voice speak these words over me was encouraging. It was the first glimpse of Jesus' plan for my new future. And more would be revealed in the coming few days.

Christine applied another dose to Suzanne's IV and checked all her vitals. The doses were about every two hours now. Staring at the telemonitor, she said, "She's running a marathon. Has been all day."

Suzanne was motionless, despite her heart rate being at a steady 145 bpm. Oxygen still hissing, readout still 92%.

Christine continued, "She's working hard. I don't know how much longer she can keep this pace, but she is comfortable." She delicately told us the process was nearing its conclusion.

After a pause, Christine looked directly at Betsy and me. In an unemotional medical tone, she said, "Her organs will start pulling blood toward them. Less blood will be available for her legs, feet, arms, and hands. You will notice her extremities will start to get cold."

It was simply a fact of how the body reacts. Betsy and I instinctively pulled a blanket over her legs and arms. We held her hands under the blanket. I appreciated Christine's guidance; it reminded Betsy and me that we were part of this process as Christine helped Suzanne. I marveled at her skill and composure. Again, I thanked Jesus for putting Christine on duty.

"You're doing this the right way, you know. I mean no resuscitation. Did you make that decision recently?"

My mind flashed back to 1980 when I entered active duty in the Air Force after Vietnam ended. The old sergeant said I needed a will. Several years later, when the kids were in school, we learned about living wills. I realized how glad I was that Suzanne and I had had those hard discussions with our lawyer when the kids were young. All the lawyer's questions were tough to consider. "What do you want to happen if you both die together, like in an airplane crash?"

We got a cold chill and looked at each other. Suzanne bristled answering all the terrible situational questions: "What if your husband is incapacitated? Do you want to let him die naturally or put him on life support, and do you want to have to decide to pull the plug?"

Suzanne and I did not like thinking about either one of us dying, and we had never considered both dying at the same time. The thought of leaving the kids alone made us both weep. They were so young. We could only perceive them in elementary school, never thought about them becoming adults.

The process, although necessary, was worse than a trip to the dentist or taking a lifestyle polygraph. And then I realized, it was one of the many great choices we made together.

Years later we established a trust to handle our estate once we were gone, actually once I was gone. Our lawyer created a living will with an advanced care directive. We didn't want to make each other, or our kids, to make hard decisions when either of us were close to death. The process was easier each time we updated the documents.

Thinking back, I could not imagine having to make those decisions as I was with her in the ICU room. My thoughts would have been taken away from that special time we had together. We only had forty-eight hours; if I had not completed all the documents beforehand, I would be doing it now. And it would have robbed me of the last forty-eight hours with Suzanne. How many hours would I have wasted researching advance care directives and talking to the nurses? It would have been horrific if I could not be by Suzanne's side, comforting her, as she passed away. I shudder to think of all the time that would have been stolen from my last hours with her.

I responded to Christine, "Yes, we made that decision a long time ago."

Christine smiled. "That's the way it's supposed to be. Let God handle it. So many people try to resuscitate their loved ones. Even though the person can't speak, they know what's going on. They still have feelings; they can still experience pain. Resuscitating a person is a terrible physical shock to put a person through. The person is dying, and to keep attempting to resuscitate their loved one is hard on the human body. And sadly, most people do it for themselves. They are selfish. They don't think about the person who is dying."

Another life lesson from Christine. I never thought about it before, but I knew she was right. The thought of putting Suzanne through that resuscitation process gave me a sick feeling all over.

The soft worship music continued to play in Christine's room. Three nurses walked into the room.

"We're going to give her a bath; we want her to be comfortable."

I was stunned at the empathy and care the nurses were showing this woman they had met only six days before today. Christine looked at me and smiled. I never figured out the hand signals or secret messages these nurses used to communicate, but the CIA could learn some things from them.

Betsy and I walked out of the room. I continued thinking about these nurses. They want her to feel good? Bathe Suzanne? Remarkable ladies.

Betsy and I took a break. We talked with a few of the nurses at their station. They looked at us, and I could tell they didn't know what to say. They knew exactly what was happening, but somehow this time it bothered them emotionally. Perhaps Suzanne had touched them as I learned before.

We saw Christine in the hall, and she waved to us to come back. We came back in, sat back down, and held Suzanne's hands some more. As Betsy and I settled, Christine said, "You're doing this right. You will get a gift."

Another clue on this journey. She had a confident, positive smile as she looked us in the eye. "Yes, you will receive a gift. She [Suzanne] must be so happy you are here."

The word "gift" continued to spin in my brain. How could we get a gift on a day like this? I believed her, even though I didn't understand. Sometimes when a person gives you a truth, it goes straight into your heart, and you immediately know it's true, even when it doesn't make any sense. This was one of the times.

The injections continued as Suzanne rested silently. She showed no evidence of stress or dismay, and Christine moved her often to ensure she was comfortable. My best friend was still running a steady marathon at 145 bpm, as 92% became 88%. It didn't impact me like I thought it would, just another passing road sign on our journey.

I realized the journey would be shorter than I previously expected, and I was so thankful to be there by her side for this last ride. Thankful to be part of every step. Grateful for everything. Especially for Jesus protecting my heart and keeping me in battle mode.

Betsy continued checking on Suzanne. As I stood to take a break, Betsy said, “Dad … she’s turning blue.”

I looked back and saw Suzanne’s legs had begun to turn a light shade of pale blue. Another road sign. I sat and held Suzanne’s hand. Betsy put the sheet and a light blanket over Suzanne’s legs and rubbed her legs to keep her warm.

Suzanne always hated to be cold, I thought.

Christine put another blanket over her legs. I wanted to be the tough, brave man, but I knew I was being held together by these two strong women, Betsy and Christine. And Jesus was holding all of us together on the inside. I wasn’t numb; I was full-on ready and calm at the same time. It was all about Suzanne now.

And I reflected and remembered it always was about Suzanne, since I met her. It was natural to be here now, as I would have it no other way. I would never leave her side. I had put all my treasure in Suzanne and never regretted it for a second. The love bank had been filled for the last forty-eight years, and the faith bank was filled to capacity. Now I was drawing on those deposits, and clearly those deposits had benefited from compounded interest over almost five decades, because I knew somehow, I would not run out of love or faith. Jesus was keeping both banks full. That’s real love right there. Love I didn’t deserve. Love I didn’t earn. Jesus provided His supernatural love.

Love that was given freely only because I met Him at a sunrise service on Easter Sunday in 1978 at SeaWorld in Orlando, Florida. I remember sitting in the stands as the sun rose, with Suzanne sitting next to me. The pastor’s voice cut across the bright, clear Florida sky as he gave the audience an invitation to accept Jesus into their heart. Memories flooded into my mind as I thought about that time. Later that day, Suzanne was concerned. She said I had changed and that we would probably break up, which made her cry. In my heart, I knew that wouldn't happen. I believe Jesus gave me a bit of confidence that He would call her too. And it was much sooner than I could have expected.

Suzanne met Jesus two weeks later at First Baptist Church in Orlando. At the end of the service, when Brother Jim gave the invitation to come forward, she quickly stood up and moved in front of me to step into the aisle. She didn't look at me or speak to me—she was looking for Jesus. As she walked forward, tears of joy streaked across my cheeks. Jesus was good.

A month later, we were at First Baptist, wearing white gowns, waiting to be baptized. Brother Jim baptized me first, then I stepped out of the baptismal and turned around. I watched Suzanne step into the baptismal. Pastor Jim spoke the words, "Based upon your profession of faith in the Lord Jesus Christ, I now baptize you, Suzanne Purifoy, in the name of the Father and the Son and Holy Ghost." I can still see her smiling at me as she stood in the baptismal. Her hair and white gown were soaked after being baptized, but she was as happy as I had ever seen her. It's funny how I don't remember what we did before or after we were baptized, and I will never forget that specific moment. The visual video is etched into my memory.

My focus returned to the hospital room. Resting on her bed, Suzanne didn't move as she continued to run the marathon. The worship music played softly in the background.

Christine continued to tell us about the next phases Suzanne would go through. Her voice was always calm and comforting. It was remarkable how a total stranger could quickly become a trusted friend. Again, I was thankful to Jesus for putting Christine with us that day.

The injections into the IV were more frequent now than before. I didn't understand how Christine knew when to administer each dose, and I wondered how many times before she had been in this situation. She was so young and so capable; her confidence in herself and her craft put me at ease.

A beep from Suzanne's monitor pierced the air, shocking me back to the reality of the situation. The key number I was constantly watching was lower. I don't remember the actual number; I knew it was lower than it should have been. And at this point, the number was displayed in yellow, no longer green. Christine reached over and turned the alarm off, permanently. The monitor still reported all the numbers and the flowing lines, but there would be no more beeps. Another road sign passed by.

Christine stayed in her room with us. Typically, she would pause and talk with us and then leave to attend to her other patients. But now she stayed and stood at the back of the room. Waiting. Several minutes passed.

Suddenly, the numbers started to fall, slowly. Numbers turned yellow, then red. No alarms. The lines slowly flattened as I watched the monitor. The road signs were passing by quickly. Almost to a blur.

I looked at Christine. She glanced at me with no expression, then watched the monitor. My eyes were glued to the monitor. I knew what was happening, but Jesus protected my heart. All I thought about was Suzanne as she finished running the marathon.

Then, all the numbers were zero. All the lines were flat. Christine reached over and turned off the monitor screen altogether.

I was sitting on Suzanne's left side, still holding her hand. Tears streamed down my cheeks.

Then I heard Betsy say, "Dad, I have this joy in my heart."

I was stunned; I, too, was feeling this sense of joy, a happiness I had never experienced. I did not understand it.

"Betsy, I'm glad you said that, because I feel it too. I didn't know how to tell you because I knew you would think I was crazy."

This was hard to believe. How could I have experienced the most dreaded, horrific event of my life, my wife dying? But somehow, I knew she was in Heaven. I didn't hear or see anything occur. I knew in my soul that the angels had jumped her to Heaven. Betsy said she knew it too.

In my worst possible nightmare, Jesus was there carrying Betsy, Matt, and I through it. I knew in an instant it was all true: all the Bible stories, all the sermons, all the Scriptures, all the gospel songs I ever heard. They were all TRUE. Even though I believed this most of my life, it became a fire in my soul like never before. I had complete confidence. God became so real to me in that instant, and I was overwhelmed with God's love. I now understand the difference between "happiness" and "joy." The deep joy that only Jesus can provide.

Christine was right: we got the "gift" of Jesus' peace, love and joy. A gift I will never lose, and one that will guide me for the rest of my life.

I stood admiring Suzanne. The woman who shaped my entire being for the last forty-eight years. This woman was the only person in my life to truly love me. This woman who made me so happy and brought unlimited joy, who made life worth living. This woman who made me smile and would make me smile the rest of my life, even though I couldn't physically see her anymore. She was so beautiful. My spirit suddenly soared. All that faith and love carried me in that instant. Jesus carried me, showing how much He loved me and her at that time. Death is only a door; it's not the end.

I kissed Suzanne's forehead. Then, I thanked Christine and the other nurses who entered the room. Betsy and I left, walking to the waiting room. One of the nurses told me that the head nurse would be in soon to help us with the next steps. Again, my mind went back to the gravity of the situation. Was I really here to discuss my wife's death? She was still so alive in my heart. The door opened, and a nurse walked in holding a folder. She was the same charge nurse I had talked to two days prior, Rebecca

My thoughts returned to the present as I readied myself for what was next. Rebecca opened the folder and smiled at me. A simple smile that appeared to convey, *I know. She's in Heaven.* Quickly, she presented the information she must have done many times before. Her training kicked in, and she explained the hospital procedures and legal requirements of the state of South Carolina. All the information was necessary and helpful, but they were only words.

I realized I was signing forms to transfer her body to the funeral home. I understood the next steps for obtaining a death certificate. She was thorough and clear, and I appreciated her professionalism. When she stopped speaking, I asked her to recommend a funeral home, which she said she wasn't allowed to do. Then the nurse side of her paused, and she said kindly, "I would send my family to Stuhr. They are good people."

I so appreciated her trusting me with that information. We all exchanged pleasantries, and I put the folder under my arm.

Betsy and I didn't say much as we walked across the hallway. I was in the hospital for a few seconds and weeks all at once. As we walked outside into a gorgeous sunny day, I looked at the sky, wondering what Suzanne was thinking and seeing. I imagined her hugging Jesus tightly around His neck with tears streaming down her cheeks. Her eyes were bright and shining. Tears now ran down my cheeks at this thought. Tears of joy that Jesus had done exactly what He promised in the Bible. She was in paradise with Him. It gave me indescribable joy, and that joy stays with me today, years later. I knew the Lord was now holding my hand as I moved forward.

Small, bright, fluffy clouds dotted the sky and drifted west as the wind blew through the trees. The temperature was in the upper fifties with low humidity, warm on this thirteenth day of December. I didn't miss the snow this time of year in northern Virginia, and neither did Suzanne. She loved South Carolina and said living here was "surreal." I was so grateful the Lord guided her and me to Charleston.

As I walked to my car, I turned and took one more look at the hospital. Opening the car door, I slid into the driver's seat, still not fully grasping the events of the past six days. I didn't realize it, but my next adventure was just beginning.

PART 3

THRIVING

ELEVEN

Moving Forward

This chapter provides a chronology of the actions I took to grieve and navigate in this new phase of my life. I am not claiming I took the right actions at the best possible times. This is just my story as I struggled to build a new life. I offer this only as an example of one man's journey.

December 14 – 31, 2022

Wisdom from Others Encouraged Me

I continued to update my journal at least once a day, and typically several times daily. Whenever I woke in the middle of the night, which was often, I captured my thoughts in the journal. This chronology helped me understand what I was experiencing, and assess how well I was progressing in my grief. In addition to my writing, I taped encouraging emails, texts, and photographs from friends on the notebook paper pages. I included powerful words from pastors, quotes, and comments from well-wishers. The journal was a key tool in shaping my new life.

Many things I was told I was unable to comprehend in the early days, but later they illuminated new truths. I accepted the wisdom and knowledge comments from others. Comments such as these inspired me to accept my situation, trust Jesus' plan, and move forward quickly with purpose.

"*One day, all of this hurt will be a memory of how your new life started.*"

"*God doesn't need us to understand or say why. We just need to find God. Have the courage to tell everyone (your story). Always be thankful and grateful.*"

"*Remember, we [believers] have more time in front of us with loved ones than without.*"

"*Everyone needs time for affirmation. Sometimes it can be simple, like a special sunset, sometimes it's a significant emotional event, like a birth or a death. God knows we need reminders, and He can use many different times in our lives to provide affirmation moments. I'm happy to know that He's turned your loss into something beautiful.*"

My sister, Bonnie, texted me a message, which was quite impactful;

"*I am a firm believer that we go through these events not to harden us, but to soften our hearts and strengthen our resolve. It's what makes us move from the comfortable to a place where we can learn how to help a fellow man in their time of need, and in turn, it feeds us. You have all the tools because she helped you gather them. You have all the lessons because she has been teaching them. It's your turn to put them to work.*"

My journal helped me identify and understand my thought process. It also helped me progress in my new life by establishing a timeline.

***

The remainder of this chapter flows chronologically based on my journal notes.

The moment when Suzanne made the jump, I received the gift of joy and peace. I accepted Jesus' plan, even though I didn't know the plan. I chose to trust Him completely, because I knew He was the only way forward for my new life. This choice allowed me to bypass the shock and denial, pain, guilt, anger, bargaining, and depression phases in grief.

I witnessed many people stuck in the early phases of grief, and I refused to let it happen to me. But sorrow approached me often. If I chose to nurture sorrow, it would lead to self-pity and ultimately deep depression that would sidetrack my new life.

I learned that sorrow is synonymous with anguish, agony, depression, misery, and torture. None of those would be allowed in my life; I chose joy over sorrow.

I wrote one phrase that kept ringing in my head on notepad paper, CHOOSE LOVE, CHOOSE JOY, and posted it on my kitchen pantry door where I could see it all day. When sorrow visited, I spoke those words out loud, adding CHOOSE JESUS. I praised Jesus for all things in my past, and, more importantly, for the future He wants me to pursue. I didn't know the target, but I knew the direction. That piece of notepad paper still hangs on my kitchen pantry door today.

Suffering is a Gift

For my entire life, I was the guy who said suffering was part of a believer's life, and it would make people wiser. But, deep inside, I never wanted to suffer and certainly did not want Suzanne to suffer. I tried to convince myself that if I lived a good life following Jesus and tried being a good husband and father, that Jesus might give me a pass. Suffering day to day working for a cruel boss or commuting two hours each way to Washington, DC, should suffice. Career changes and the ups and downs of raising kids aren't suffering as much as I wanted them to be counted. Real suffering started when Suzanne was admitted to the hospital. It was a journey I did not expect and one I didn't believe I was prepared to handle.

I searched for help to move forward. Seacoast Church sponsored the nationwide Christian-based Grief Share program that teaches how to move from mourning to joy. I registered, but it was a month before the thirteen-week program started. Searching the Internet, I purchased a Grief Share book, *God's Healing for Life's Losses* by Dr. Robert Kellemen. It was in this book that I learned suffering should bring us closer to God; it opens our hands to God. Similarly, Augustine of Hippo (of St Augustine, Florida, fame) wrote in the year 426, "God is always trying to give good things to us, but our hands are too full to receive them" in *City of God*, Penguin Books, November 27, 2003.

I realized suffering was bringing me closer to Jesus, and that gave me a new perspective on what is really important in life. I believe suffering connects us all; suffering is a gift in some ways. It taught me to do the hard things in life, and Jesus showed me love and guided me through grief. I also learned I can have pain and joy in my life *simultaneously*, thanks to Katherine Wolf, who explained this truth in *Suffer Strong: How to Survive Anything by Redefining Everything,* Thomas Nelson, February 11, 2020.

January 2023

Proud Celebration

We held the Celebration of Life for Suzanne on January 25, 2023. The chapel filled with friends, old and new. One of the worship leaders, Natasha Gray[3], blessed us with her beautiful voice singing the songs Suzanne requested plus *Available*[4], which I selected based on Morris Morrison's recommendation since I was now retired and single, thus available to serve the Lord. That day, I was never prouder to be Suzanne's husband and tell our story, while praising Jesus for the last 48 years.

After the service, Bonnie handed me a bound sketch book. Inside the cover she wrote "Go buy yourself some charcoal pencils, another radiograph, a set of Prismacolors, some decent water colors, quality brushes (fine and broad), and a gum eraser. Life is waiting for you!" Her suggestion to return to my first love, art, gave me the initial step in building a new life.

As I reflected on our last week together in December, I realized that Suzane never complained about her situation. She never got mad at God, broke down in tears or blamed anyone. She simply trusted God. I need a faith like hers.

Spiritual Vision Focuses Building My New Life

Four days after Suzanne's celebration of life service, I attended Sunday services on January 29, 2023 at Seacoast Church with family and friends. The service opened with a video of a Seacoast Church trip to Israel. The narration started, "He gets to use us however He wants. It's all about His will, His purposes, His glory. And if we are going to serve Him, we have to have that perspective."

My mind held fast to these words; in my heart, I knew it was true. Following the video, Joel presented the message, stating that goals are difficult to achieve unless you have a vision, and a spiritual vision is key. His explanation of spiritual vision inspired me:

> *Let's define spiritual vision; it's a clarity of purpose and commitment to follow the leading of God in my life. Spiritual vision beats goals every single day. Spiritual vision will help you see joy when others see sorrow and pain. Spiritual vision will help you gain strength when everything about you should say you are feeling weak. And when you get a vision for something, you can do what others see as impossible.*

Joel's words helped me understand the joy and strength I was experiencing. Focusing on Jesus was the answer, as always. Helping others was the way forward for me. I captured my thoughts about spiritual vision in my journal over the next few weeks after Suzanne's passing. My spiritual vision would explain my "why" on the afternoon of December 13, 2022; I needed to serve Jesus fully and be grateful for Suzanne and Him. My spiritual vision burned in my heart and became a driving force for my new life. Next, I needed to define "what" I needed to do to implement my spiritual vision.

In the last week of January, I documented my "what"; *I will be more engaged in spreading the good news of the Gospel using my unique God-given talents. I will never leave a void by not using these talents. I will not fail this mission, and I'm ALL IN.*

The next step in implementing my "why" was to determine "how." Making random notes in my journal as I thought and prayed revealed the start of the answer by the end of the week.

On the evening of January 31, 2023, I grabbed a piece of printer paper and a black gel pen and drew circles filled with thoughts on goals. I summarized potential goals for serving the Lord using the unique gifts and skills He had given me. Then I grouped each of the goals to focus and shape them into tasks. After several attempts that evening, by midnight, I had captured my goals on a single sheet of paper to identify "how" to achieve my spiritual vision.

The next step was to determine "when" I needed to take action on each goal. I prioritized my goals by their potential impact and the time required to achieve each goal. With this high-level timeframe, I added detail on "when" to achieve each goal. Tying my why, what, how, and when together created a living plan that would flux as priorities and resources changed and new ideas emerged.

In my military career, I learned that the first 5% of time in any project should be dedicated to planning because it drives the remaining 95% of the project implementation. I estimated at least 20 years remained for me to be productive in my new life; that's 7,300 days, and 5% of that is 365 days to build and start my new life plan. I also needed to track progress, and the lack of it, to replan effectively. It would take three months to complete the first draft plan and schedule to achieve the goals in pursuit of the spiritual vision.

The plan gave me a well-defined path, worth the time and effort. My plan gave me hope: it also gave me a future, a way to pay forward all the love Suzanne gave to me, and to serve Jesus, who gave us both a lifetime of love on earth and an eternity in Heaven.

Created a Kingdom (of God) Perspective

Before December 2022, my perspective focused primarily on our lives together, with not much thought about Heaven, because that's only the place you end up. I considered my relationship with Jesus to be good and consistent. Jesus was always core in my worldview, and I saw Him in everyday life. I didn't think about Heaven often, mostly because I didn't understand it. I never believed Heaven was cute with tiny angels playing harps on clouds; it was a wonderful place where we go after death. I was happy on earth and didn't need to consider it yet. In January 2023, I started reading *Heaven* by Randy Alcorn, pastor of Eternal Perspective Ministries, and I got excited about Heaven for the first time in my life.

Learning that we will know each other with intact memories of our earthly lives quickly changed my perspective. Realizing that God created us each uniquely and that we will be with Him in His Kingdom on the new earth shifted my paradigm. I viewed my time on earth as much smaller, not less important, only less significant. My view of Heaven became bigger and more realistic.

I knew deep in my soul Suzanne was there, as were many other loved ones. She was worth every minute I put into our relationship, and she changed me and my life for the better. She had been my best friend for the last forty-eight years. I always loved her and will always be eternally grateful to her.

I hope that when I see her again, she will say, "Lee, I am proud of you! You didn't waste time; you made a difference." I understand more than ever the importance of telling others about Jesus so He can call and lead them to salvation.

After her last day with me, I now see death as a door. It may appear to be an end, but it's really a transition from this life on earth to eternal life in Heaven. God numbers our days from the start of our lives, and every day is a gift. Although the time before I join her may be a few decades for me, that's not even one second of time in Heaven. And the perspective of the Kingdom is important for me to retain as I move forward.

Heaven became my goal line, my planned destination. I know it's there, and it helped me understand the drive in my heart to do all I can to make a difference before I get there. Earth time seems so brief now. My daily perspective is much different, as all that really matters is loving God and loving people. Typical life issues don't seem as significant as Heaven is always in my forward-looking view now. I live daily on earth, and my heart is focused on Heaven. I live in two realms.

Never Considered Myself a Victim

Throughout this process, and for all my life, I never considered myself a victim. In the grieving process, I learned it was my responsibility to maintain a positive attitude to keep living, avoiding self-pity and victimhood. There were times I would drift into feeling sorry for myself, but I self-corrected as quickly as possible. If I allowed myself to go the negative route, it would become a downward spiral that I might not be able to recover from in the future. I would have none of that, as I had too much to accomplish. Of course, there were emotional days in the beginning, but I pressed forward, and now they are gone.

Faith was the major contributor to my positive attitude and the joy I lived in every day. And the joy of the Lord remains the consistent answer.

February 2023

Alone

In the middle of February, I realized I was really alone and needed to start building a new life. For a couple weeks, I was overcome with sadness that Suzanne was never coming home, and that she no longer needed me. And I really needed her. More importantly, I need to find my way forward. Only forward, never back.

March 2023

Moved from Fear to Freedom Quickly

After being with Suzanne for almost five decades, our lives were completely intertwined. We talked constantly and did everything together, mostly because it was more enjoyable. We shared the typical household tasks like cooking, cleaning, laundry, mowing the lawn, and maintaining the house. We took turns buying groceries and household goods. Together, we shopped for clothes, cars, furniture, and scrapbook supplies. We got a few strange looks in stores because we always held hands, no matter how old we were.

Then, suddenly, I was alone. The simple task of buying groceries became cumbersome to me, as I now had to make the shopping list, I had to decide what to cook, and I needed to know the expiration dates on products. And that was the easy part.

On the first few trips to the grocery store, I sat in the car with tears in my eyes. I didn't know how to simply walk in without Suzanne. I drove back to my house without going in.

On my next trip, I went late in the evening so few people would be there and not seeing me walking through the aisles with tears in my eyes. I made multiple trips across all the aisles because I didn't know where anything was in the store. I used to push the cart while Suzanne led the way. It took a couple of trips to complete one week's worth of shopping. But on each subsequent trip, it got easier.

The first time I went to the hardware store, I experienced the same emotions. Although each first was emotional, there would only be one first time for each task. After the first, I had broken through my fear. I realized that if I was going to make it, I needed to face my fears head-on. More importantly, I recognized that the faster I approached and beat each of my fears, the sooner I would be able to live in freedom in my new life.

If Suzanne could have talked to me, she would have said, "*Get your butt in there and get going, do what you gotta do, Lee!*"

I played her voice in my head whenever I experienced fear over everyday tasks, and it worked like a charm. I actually started going places to complete that first trip. Soon I was walking out away with a smile on my face, because I "did what I had to do." And the fear and discomfort quickly evaporated, never to return. I was living in freedom.

By the end of the first year after Suzanne's death, I had completed about sixty percent of the tasks in my new life plan. Even though sixty percent is a failing grade, I was proud of my progress. I completed all time-critical tasks and those of a lower priority. The forty percent not completed included tasks with unrealistic schedules or resources and tasks I never needed to accomplish. Most importantly, I saw progress regularly, which helped me move forward.

April 2023

God Has a Plan

During my daily prayer time on April 5, the Holy Spirit spoke to my heart, telling me He had a plan for my new life. I didn't understand it initially, but I decided to move forward in expectation. I always believed the future, although unknown, holds unlimited new opportunities for the believer. I chose to put my belief into action.

Wisdom from Grief Share Attendees

During table discussions on Tuesday evenings, the Grief Share leaders asked us to share our insights on our personal journeys. One evening, one participant, David, stated, "I believe God is using this to make me into the person He wants me to be." His words stunned me as I realized I had a choice to make. Trust God and move forward or ignore God and become stagnant.

On another evening, another participant, Holly, recalled insights from a friend. She drew a box on a piece of white printer paper, saying, "This is us." Then she drew a circle that filled the box and called it our grief. She added, "We can't make our grief smaller; we have to add new things to our lives to make the box bigger so the grief will be smaller in us." She drew the box bigger. Immediately, I understood and chose to make my box bigger; it was the only way to proceed.

Quickly Established a New Identity

Perhaps the most significant aspect of the Grief Share program was its recommendation to create a new identity for myself. As a single man, my interests, friends, and activities would change regardless of my actions. Since they were going to change, I decided to define and manage that change in the direction of my choosing.

As soon as I became a widower, people weren't sure how to talk to me. They didn't want to hurt my feelings by saying the wrong thing. I realized my friends' perception of me had changed, and I needed to help them navigate how to interact with me. Also, I needed new activities and interests to discuss instead of the passing of my wife.

Our physical appearance is one way we all communicate. I've heard that 80% of a person's perception of someone is how that person looks, and only 20% of what they say. Our brains rely primarily on vision to understand the world we live in. If I appeared a bit different, that would immediately impact others' perception of me. If I became disheveled, their thoughts would go in one direction, and the opposite would be true.

Changing my wardrobe also forced me to develop a new style and learn how to dress accordingly. It definitely was time for a change, and I searched for answers. YouTube and department store websites gave me a few tips. All I needed to do was match the many photos they displayed. The best resources were salesmen in quality men's stores. They knew the current trends, what was appropriate for my age, and what styles fit me the best. I listened to them, handed them my credit card, and was never disappointed.

The new attire affected my mental state positively. Wearing something different and new built my confidence in public. My new attire style was working, but I knew I needed to do something different.

Since I grew up during the disco era, spending unending nights on lighted dance floors, I figured I had nothing to lose. I contacted the Arthur Murray dance studio in town, whose owner, JR, explained they use a rigorous curriculum to teach dance with testing and frequent practices. For the first few months, I didn't tell anyone—including my kids—that I had joined. Learning was quite slow in the beginning, but my dance instructor, AnneMarie, was patient and talented. Eventually, I learned the initial phases of six dances and enjoyed every minute of it. Despite being the oldest guy there, all the other dancers were welcoming and delightful. It's one of the most wholesome and energetic things a person can do. And I learned few men know how to dance, and most women not only can dance but want to dance, which sealed the deal for me.

Since dance was so enjoyable, I decided to try some new hobbies. My sister encouraged me to return to my first love—art. Taking her advice, I visited Hobby Lobby and bought acrylic paint, canvases, and paint brushes of all sizes. Over forty years had passed since I quit art in college, but I jumped in. Once again, YouTube was my teacher as I wasted a lot of paint and ruined a few canvases. Discovery is a good thing for the brain, and I was creating new neural pathways.

My kids were supportive even though I knew they weren't completely truthful about some of my masterpieces which were actual disasters.

New hobbies and buying a new car were positive changes in building my new life, but the most rewarding was getting more involved in serving at church and helping people. For me, the best way not to dwell on my situation was to focus on others. Serving at my church and helping others resulted in improving my perspective and attitude. Volunteering in an area that touched my heart was one of the best ways to continue moving forward in my grief.

My main point here is that it didn't really matter what I did differently if I made changes and learned something new. Meeting new people and new activities brought joy. Clearing out all the old things I no longer used was liberating. Many of the artifacts I thought were wonderful memories were actually millstones, and out they went.

I rarely turned on my television and eventually canceled my Cable TV subscription, and I haven't missed it.

I hope you realize how much you have to offer the world, so be a part of it, and live life to the fullest.

May 2023

Stay Close to Jesus

In the midst of praying, I felt the Holy Spirit communicate to me, "Let nothing come between us, Lee." I paused and knew immediately I needed to comply. It solidified my belief I was on the right track and needed to ensure I didn't drift away from God.

As painful and lonesome as life was at times, I knew my time alone would transition me to my new life; allow me to look back and appreciate Suzanne; and make me draw closer to Jesus, to learn more.

June 2023

Changed My Home Environment

"Don't make any major decisions in the first year" was guidance from Grief Share, friends, and books. I liked my house and decided to stay for a couple of years. Since I was going to stay, I wanted a fresh, masculine style for the house. New paint would help and would be attractive to a buyer. I hired my favorite contractor to paint the entire interior. Before he arrived, I removed about ninety percent of the wall coverings to start the new style. The painters spread out two weeks of work into three weeks because Charleston had record heat, and the painters were happy to be in the air conditioning. When the painting was complete, I decided to make more changes to make it "my home."

Since I spent a majority of my time in the living room, I updated the furniture and color scheme to create a more masculine feel. Most of the other furniture in the house would stay, I decided, at least for now.

We had two bedrooms upstairs that were not useful as bedrooms in my new life. I changed one into a guest room with new modern furniture and wall hangings that would welcome family and friends. The other bedroom became an art studio with easels, canvas racks, and wood flooring. Topping it off, I added a rebuilt 1973 Marantz receiver and turntable. I continued to waste paint and ruin canvases, but I didn't care. My paintings started to cover the empty walls, and dripped paint covered the wood floor

Replacing the master bedroom furniture resulted in the biggest emotional uplift. I flipped the color scheme in the opposite direction and added paintings and plants. It became my room.

I always enjoyed being outdoors and swimming in the pool in the backyard. But the neighbors on both sides had large dogs that barked at my dogs every chance they could. To remedy that situation, I installed a large wooden privacy fence and new shrubs; it completely changed the feel of the backyard for the better and no more barking mongrels. And whenever I sold the house, this addition would be a positive selling point.

In addition to changing the house, it was time to change me. I documented a plan to exercise, eat healthy, minimize stress, increase vitamin intake, and get better and more sleep. It not only got me out of the house, but it made positive difference in my attitude and outlook.

Freedom Program Reinforces God's Love

Based on recommendations from friends, I started the ten-week "Freedom" program at Seacoast. Freedom was developed by the Church of the Highlands in Birmingham, Alabama, to build on the foundation of faith in Christ. It focused on embracing the truth of God's Word as it related to my personal worldview, my value to God, and my purpose in His kingdom. Upon completion, I better understood God's love for all of us, and it helped me to walk in freedom in my new life.

Learned to Live Solo with Joy in My Heart

Since I only had forty-eight hours with Suzanne in the hospital after her diagnosis, friends and family were caught by surprise and set up no support process typical of a lengthy terminal illness. In addition, it was the Christmas season, with most people preparing for the holidays, and their normal routines were on hold. This situation forced me to fend for myself, although I didn't think about it as a negative. One does what one has to do.

I started doing everything myself and established a new weekly routine for cooking, cleaning, laundry, shopping, and the like. YouTube became my favorite resource and teacher, and I can now brag to my friends about separating laundry for whites and colors and using cold, warm, and hot water. The ladies claimed to be impressed, while the guys thought I lost my mind.

Actually, the process helped me find it. I decided not to tell anyone about the time I washed a new red shirt with other clothes, so that can be our secret. However, I still don't understand how to use bleach effectively in the laundry. And why are there so many different kinds of bleach?

YouTube let me down on ironing dress shirts. Never could figure out the correct way the ironing board should face, spray starch is a mess, and incorrect iron settings resulted in a few scorched shirts. My dry-cleaning lady advised me on what clothes needed dry cleaning or laundering, and when to use starch (there's more than one option I learned) and creases. Life became easier when I asked the experts for advice.

Cooking outdoors was one of my few skills that I excelled at—assuming you like well-done—but cooking in the kitchen was a new challenge. I learned the value of a grocery shopping list, coupons, and buy-one-get-one-free items. I made friends with the staff at Publix, who were kind enough to give me advice. Thanks to YouTube and the staff at Coastal Cupboard, I learned how to cook with the gas cooktop and the electric oven, not only the microwave. They showed me how to season a cast-iron skillet and the stainless-steel pans I purchased. I subscribed to the *Southern Living* magazine and their emails that provide recipes with a limited number of ingredients. So far, there have been no kitchen fires, although a few of my meals would scare a possum away.

When Suzanne and I moved to Charleston, I worked from home, which provided more free time to help her. Being at home all day, I learned her routine for cleaning the house. I wanted to have fun with her and realized that if I helped clean the house every week, that would give her more free time for me. She reluctantly agreed with a bit of panic on her face. I tried to read her mind and decided she was thinking, *He is going to break everything (as I had done before) or he won't really follow through.*

Suzanne decided to give me a chance and taught me the difference between a weekly clean and a monthly deep clean. It was time well spent, and I soon learned that maintaining the home significantly helped me maintain a positive attitude. She always kept the house straight, and now that I was doing it, I gained a new sense of pride.

Through all of this, I gained independence and more self-respect. I always did the monthly home maintenance, and now I know how to do all the other tasks. It was like building a new muscle; it's hard at first, but the more you work at it, the better you become and the easier it gets. I also had no idea how much time all of these home tasks required and was impressed that Suzanne did it for years with ease and never complained. She made it seem easy.

Learned How to Be Alone, But Never Lonely

The initial days at home by myself were a challenge after living with Suzanne for over four decades. I used my new daily routine to stay on track with the housework. During the week, I was busy at Seacoast Church and starting new hobbies. But in the evenings, the house was quiet, and the winter sun set early.

Reading at night and taking evening convertible rides helped offset this new feeling of loneliness. As I continued to reflect on what I was feeling, I realized loneliness was connected to being abandoned or having no friends and limited contact with others. This was not the case, and I needed to accept being alone, but not lonely. It meant I was single now and needed to rely more on friends and family.

As I continued to ponder my situation, I searched online for synonyms for "lonely." What I found shocked me: anguish, agony, depression, despair, gloom, Hell, misery, and pain. When I saw Hell associated with lonely, I knew what I needed to do.

Realized Banking Love and Faith Helped Me Survive Her Death, then Thrive in My New Life

For over forty-eight years, Suzanne and I grew our love. I don't think there's a fast microwave option for love; it takes time. It's simple and complex all at once. Concepts are easy, and the daily implementation can be challenging but always rewarding. We learned about life together, gaining new knowledge individually. All of this blended together and strengthened our love. The more we focused on each other, the more Jesus made His love flow between us.

I recently realized all those years we were building a love "bank." It was a new concept to me that I created, thinking about what happened on her last day on earth. I realize that we had been investing and drawing on that love bank our entire marriage.

When we hit some challenges with family and work, we drew on that love bank. We always filled it, but I don't think it was intentional. We put each other first and let go of issues that didn't really matter.

I had learned early in our marriage to lose the argument and win the marriage. And the few times we disagreed; it was so trivial it really didn't matter to me. And most of the time, it was me who said something insensitive or forgot her birthday. To this day, I honestly can't remember being mad at Suzanne for anything.

True forgiveness worked like that in our marriage. Between us, it was always forgive and forget. And we never brought anything forward from the past. It was the love bank filled to capacity that carried her and me through that week, and yes, all that love flowed directly from Jesus. I guess He's the bank president in this analogy.

And that love, continually funded by Jesus, has carried me every day since she made the jump to Heaven. I wondered recently how it could be almost two years since I have seen her, but I still have that deep, warm glow of gratitude in my heart for Suzanne. This realization that it was always His love we experienced was a bit overwhelming. How could Jesus be so gracious and kind? That type of supernatural love is not possible between a human husband and wife without Jesus. It was Him, always Him.

I knew above all else it was Jesus in our lives all the time. It was the amazing lessons and truths written in the Bible. The amazing stories of ordinary men and women that God used to His glory. All the small groups that created a community to teach each other and share life. We always kept Jesus integral in our marriage, and it was the three of us, not two: it definitely was "we three, and not me." This simple, consistent acceptance of Jesus Christ, His teachings, His salvation, and His heavenly blessings made our life together a wonderful experience.

Suzanne was always faithful, setting the example for me. She prayed for years for certain things that never occurred in her lifetime. Perhaps disappointed at times, she never stopped believing. No complaints ever.

When her prayers were not answered, and she had to go in a different direction, she didn't lose heart. Often, she would tell me with tears in her eyes, "I asked God why He didn't answer my prayer, and He said, 'Because you can handle it.'" And with that, she accepted His answer and moved forward in peace. She never got angry at God—disappointed and sad at times, but never mad—and never turned her back on God. She was teaching me, like she always did.

Together over the years, we simply trusted and believed in Jesus. We knew He loved us and wanted the best for us individually and in our marriage, and all those years of believing and trusting were adding to our faith banks.

That's probably not a scriptural explanation, but it's my way of viewing the situation. When the worst event possible occurred to us both, I started pulling from that faith bank. And I learned that when you "bank" with Jesus, He provides overdraft protection.

Suzanne never faltered in her last days as she dealt with dying. I never faltered as I watched her die. And He didn't let either of us down; Jesus lifted us like never before in our lives. No charge for interest, nor did He expect me to pay back all the faith we withdrew. Jesus made a personal donation to our accounts, forever.

On some days, I put a penny in the love bank. Some days it was a quarter. Some days I forgot to make a deposit, and some days it was a dollar. But I continued to add to the bank, and Jesus honored my consistent, albeit erratic, method of increasing my balance in both banks. He added compounded interest to grow my accounts exponentially due only to His love. What I invested in my account was meager compared to the payments we received during our marriage, and I continue to receive them since Suzanne went home to be with Him.

Six months later, in the breezeway at Seacoast Church, I chatted with a staff member who led the Care Ministry. As we talked, my mind suddenly grabbed a core message: "***Start now, start today***."

I followed the thought thread back to Suzanne's words on Sunday morning. Tears in her eyes, struggling to accept the Stage 4 lung cancer diagnosis, she remarked, "I have no regrets. I would not change a thing," as her voice broke. I thought, *Did we do life right and not realize it*?

I started to encourage everyone who would listen to me to "Start Now" to strengthen their relationship with Jesus and their wife. Put your treasure in your wife, not your job or hobbies. Regardless of how long a couple had been married or how old they were, there was time. But there was likely less time than most imagine. Time is the only resource we use daily, despite never knowing the remaining balance. All that matters is the future, so start now. "Expect the best, plan for the worst, and prepare to be surprised" was a familiar quote that applied to my life now.

September 2023

Rooted Program Deepened My Relationship with Jesus

Based on recommendations from my Freedom program group, I started the ten-Week "Rooted" program at Seacoast Church. Rooted guided me though the seven rhythms grounded in Acts 2, which included Daily Devotion, Prayer, Repentance, Serve the Community, Sacrificial Generosity, Share Your Story, and Worship. Working through the topics with others helped baseline my walk with Jesus. It also guided me in leveraging my life to help others.

December 2023

"Survived" the First Year

The recurring annual holiday dates never affected me. I didn't anticipate or dread those events, such as my first Easter and Mother's Day alone. Never expecting to be the type of person who visits cemeteries, at the on year point I needed to visit the Veterans Administration's National Cemetery in Beaufort, South Carolina, where Suzanne was buried. The top was down on the red convertible as I drove south on that beautiful sunny day with a bright blue Carolina sky.

As I stood at Suzanne's marker, I thought about the past year. Much had changed in my life thanks to my plan pushing me forward in pursuit of my vision. Driving out of the iron gates onto Boundary Avenue, I passed Adventure Street. The warm sun lit up the tree lined streets. Suddenly, I realized I had made it. A whole year passed, and I not only survived, but I thrived.

January 2024

Updated My Plan for Year 2 and Beyond

My year one plan primarily focused on the transition to my new life. Throughout the first year, I continually adjusted tasks and schedules to stay on track with my plan. The number of tasks grew to over 300, but many were one-time efforts that would not be required after the first year. About 180 tasks were completed in year 1, and my established routine would ensure I maintained those tasks in year 2. My year 2 plan focused on living the new life and sustaining momentum toward the vision. I streamlined my plan to focus only on key goals. This change made it easier to remember the key tasks and plan updates dropped from daily to monthly.

September 2024

Unstoppable Growth Program Focuses My Spiritual Vision

Almost 2 years had passed, and it was time to plan for year 3. Although I was on track with my plan, I sensed a drive to focus on a primary outreach. One that would use my unique skills and experience. Initially, I believed it would be around my lifelong interest in art and drawing cartoons. I also considered illustrating a children's book focused on Bible truths, which is one reason I learned acrylic abstract painting. Despite good options, I was unable to focus on a primary one to drive to completion.

During my thought process, friends suggested the *Unstoppable Growth* program to focus on God's plan for my life.

In parallel with the message series on gratitude, I enrolled in the *Unstoppable Growth* program led by two pastors, Tim and Rebecca Lindsay, at Seacoast Church. Their program included a workbook and interactive sessions with the pastors and other participants. I learned to define my story at a macro level to see where God led me over my life. They helped me overcome my internal roadblocks and primary distractions. They taught me that Jesus knows my story, is not frustrated by it, and wants to write the next chapter of my story so I can share it for His glory.

The next step uncovered my why, what, and how, to show me the way to proceed. I identified our spiritual, relational, physical, intellectual, and financial capital to be leveraged in our story. The program culminated in creating a vision board to summarize my vision with supporting goals.

During the program, a young Marine commented to me, "I would love to read about those last forty-eight hours with your wife. What you did, what you talked about. That would be fascinating."

Immediately, I knew I needed to tell the story of the last 48 hours with Suzanne in the hospital and the last 48 years of our lives together. The next morning, I started writing my thoughts about those last two days with Suzanne. My journal became a rich resource of information. My cellphone was filled with photographs, each with the date and time. The story continued to expand backward to explain how we got to the last forty-eight hours and how I moved forward.

I began waking every morning at three-thirty a.m., obsessed with writing my story. I typed feverishly on my computer keyboard for three months straight. I finished the first draft on December 11, 2024.

Retelling the story required me to relive December 2022 and the initial months alone. The drive to tell my story was greater than the pain from the memories, and I pressed forward. I completed the first draft before the third anniversary of Suzanne's jump to Heaven, reflecting on all that had transpired since that day. My future is unknown with unlimited opportunities, and that excites me. I pray I will never slow on this journey.

Art Heals

I mentioned to Joel I was learning to paint again so he suggested I join the Manifold Creative Arts[6] group at Seacoast. At this point I was drafting *The Last 48* and was seeking guidance and inspiration. Nicole, who leads the group, welcomed me at the first Manifold meeting. The group members talked about a wide variety of creative arts. We discussed painting techniques, writing styles, web pages, and publishing tips. I met four authors that offered assistance. Nicole opened each meeting with a motivational message about the importance of using our artistic skills to honor Jesus.

This was the first group that made me feel welcome and I never had to talk about being a widower. It was refreshing to focus on creativity again. I realized how much I missed art since I left it in college forty-five years ago. I had no idea that blindly buying some paint and canvases months ago would lead to a whole new world with interesting people.

October 2024

Unexpected Return; New Start

Katie Walters, Seacoast's Marriage Ministry Pastor, asked me to tell my story on "Marriage Monday" at our church. I arrived early to prepare and the Chapel was empty when I walked in. The room was already prepared for the engaged and married couples. Beautiful flowers and candles adored the tables. My mind raced back to January 25, 2023. I was stunned at how my life had changed in twenty months, and I gave all praise to Jesus. Tears filled my eyes.

Soon, people began to fill the chapel as the start time neared. Everyone was kind and welcoming which made me feel like I belonged. That evening, I made new friends, including one that would be essential to my journey in my new adventure.

November 2024

Allowed Eternal Gratitude to Replace Temporary Earthly Love

Joel presented a series on gratitude on November 17th. One Sunday, Joel's words changed my paradigm on gratitude, and as he spoke, these words displayed on the screen behind him: "*Gratitude: an appreciation of what God has done, is doing, and a hope for what He will do.*[5]"

God flipped a light switch in my head. He explained what I was feeling was gratitude, not only love. And in my situation, gratitude was a stronger motivating force than love. Every song I heard about Heaven brought tears due to my gratitude for all He did for Suzanne and me and all believers. I was grateful she chose to spend the last forty-eight years with me.

Our pastor continued, and these words displayed behind him: "*Gratitude: Is an action, not an attitude.*"

Now I fully understood his message. Gratitude became the key motivator in year two and would continue driving my new life. Best of all, gratitude can withstand the test of time. I also learned it's impossible to be in a love relationship with a person no longer on this earth.

I Let Go of Her

About eighteen months had passed in my new life. I made decisions alone, still focused on Suzanne's interests because I lived for her. That focus began to feel odd as it held me to the past, and I could not break that paradigm. My close friends frequently suggested I start "doing things for me."

Initially, I didn't appreciate their wisdom. As my second Thanksgiving approached, I understood their messages. Reviewing our life together and Suzanne's departure, I remembered she was never "mine." Suzanne was on loan to me to care for and love for the last forty-eight years. She belonged only to her heavenly Father.

To succeed, I moved away from my old life and fully embraced my new life. The cornerstone of changing my paradigm was complete acceptance that Suzanne was gone from this earth, living in joy in Heaven. I needed to let go of her to move forward. She will always be a part of me, and I will always be grateful for her. But I needed to stop thinking about her so much and to focus on the future. I remembered she told me to remarry, and I need to be fully available to a new woman that the Lord places in my life. I can love only one woman at a time. So, letting go of her was an important step because I wanted love in my life again.

Continuing to Move Forward

I realized after the fact that Matt, Betsy, and I only had forty-eight hours before Suzanne made the jump. They had no warning; it hit them, and me. I remain grateful to God for giving me forty-eight hours with her and the honor of being with Suzanne when she started her new life. Some people have more than forty-eight hours but don't appreciate the gift of that special time. Some have less time and wish they had more.

The only way it worked for her and me all those years was to keep Jesus integral in our lives and marriage. We didn't need to be big names in a church or provide the largest donations. Simply trusting and growing a personal relationship with Jesus was all it took. The closer we each got to Jesus, the closer she and I got to each other. It was always the three of us, and that's all we ever needed.

So, while my story focused on Suzanne and Lee it's not really about us at all. We were two minor role players in a massive multi-generational story being orchestrated every day by God since the day He created the heavens and the earth. It's all about Jesus. It's so simple.

My story will continue to progress, as much remains to be done. My new adventure continues to unfold before me. In this season of life, I am excited to pursue all Jesus wants me to achieve. Now I realize He was training me for such a time as this.

I pray that I can leverage what I learned over the last 48 years, and those last 48 hours to help others. Because it's all about Jesus. Always.

I will continue pursuing my spiritual vision as long as He keeps me deployed on this crazy place we call Earth. I will embrace new opportunities as I run to the future.

I often wonder what happens in Heaven. Perhaps love is what Heaven is all about, pure love exchanged. The Bible explains that God sent Jesus as His expression of His love for all of us. Heaven is there for anyone who seeks Jesus' forgiveness of their sins and accepts Him as their Lord and Savior. Jesus can forgive all sins.

"May the God of hope fill you with all joy and peace as you trust in Him, so that you may overflow with hope by the power of the Holy Spirit." *Romans 15:13 (NIV)*

May 1975

Bibliography

Alcorn, Randy. *Heaven*. Tyndale, Carol Stream, IL, 2004.

Beshore, Kenton and Wanjau, Muriithi. *Rooted*; *Connect with God, The Church, Your Purpose*, Mariners Church, Irvine, CA, 2020.

Broocks, Rice & Murrell, Steve. *The Purple Book, Updated Edition: Biblical Foundations for Building Strong Disciples.* Zondervan, Grand Rapids, MI, 2017.

Buford, Bob. *Halftime*. Zondervan, Grand Rapids, MI, 1994.

Church Initiative. *Grief Share.* Church Initiative, Wake Forest, NC, 2021.

Dobson, James C. *Dare to Discipline*. Tyndale House, Wheaton, Ill, 1970.

Groeschel Craig, *Winning the War in Your Mind: Change Your Thinking, Change Your Life.* Zondervan Books, Grand Rapids, MI, 2021.

Hodges, Chris. *Freedom*. Church of the Highlands, Birmingham, AL, 2023.

Jeremiah, David. *Angels*, Multnomah Publishers, Sisters, OR, 2006.

Kellerman, Dr. Robert. *God's Healing for Life's Losses*. BMH Books, Winona Lakes, IN, 2010.

Keller, Timothy. *The Meaning of Marriage*. Penguin Random House, 2011.

Lewis, C.S. *A Grief Observed.* Harper One, New York, NY, 2015.

Lewis, C.S. *The Problem of Pain.* Harper One, New York, NY, 1996.

Lucado, Max. *Fearless: Imagine Your Life Without Fear.* Thomas Nelson, Nashville, TN, 2012.

Lindsay, Tim, and Rebecca. *Unstoppable Growth.* Amazon, Mt Pleasant, SC, 2023.

Smith, J. Josh. *The Titus Ten*. B&H Publishing, Brentwood, TN, 2020.

Wolf, Katherine and Jay. *Strong: How to Survive Anything by Redefining Everything.* Thomas Nelson, Nashville, TN, 2020.

Wright, Norman. *Reflections of a Grieving Spouse: The Unexpected Journey from Loss to Renewed Hope.* Harvest House, Eugene OR, 2009.

Acknowledgements

My deepest thanks to my friends who
helped bring my story to print, and share the passion to spread the Gospel;

Justin Brazell

Yolanda Echeverri

Jack Echeverri

Rebecca Lindsay

Tim Lindsay

John London

Joyce London

Susan Nolan

Nicole Seitz

Scot Shier

Brian Thorne

Danielle Thorne

Bridget Wells

Link to The Last 48 online resource

QR code link to *The Last 48 Book* web site that provides additional information and resources for readers

LeeCarrick.com

Endnotes

Links to music and messages in *The Last 48*;

1. *I Can Only Imagine*, Mercy Me, 2001, on Spotify

2. *The Blessing*, Kari Jobe, Cody Barnes, 2020, on Spotify

3. Natasha Gray music on Spotify

4. *Available*, Elevation Worship, 2020, on Spotify

5. Pastor Joel Delph's message on Spiritual Vision on YouTube

6. Manifold Creative Arts Ministry on Instagram

7. Pastor Joel Delph's message on Gratitude on YouTube

About the Author

Lee grew up in the sixties amidst towering pine trees, palmetto bushes that concealed reptiles, tea-colored lakes teeming with fish, alligators patrolling the lake shore, and constant sunshine in Central Florida. As a senior in high school, he met a pretty girl he would marry six years later. Lee's military career moved them coast to coast, ending at the Pentagon. Following military retirement, he served in companies in a variety of leadership roles in the defense and intelligence markets.

In preparation for full retirement, Lee and Suzanne left the fast-paced life in the Washington, DC, metropolitan area for Charleston, South Carolina. The low country was the perfect fit for 6 years until their adventure of over 48 years ended abruptly with only 48 hours' notice.

Lee's new mission is to encourage others to build strong relationships with Jesus and their spouses to live a no-regrets life. By doing so, they can enjoy their lives together and be better prepared for whatever traumatic events they face in life, including the inevitable.

www.ingramcontent.com/pod-product-compliance
Lightning Source LLC
LaVergne TN
LVHW090512110826
845146LV00003B/831

* 9 7 9 8 2 1 8 8 6 2 7 2 5 *